Programming Problems in Java

A Primer for The Technical Interview

James Wong
JAVA.ALGORITHMIST@GMAIL.COM

Bradley Green
ALGORITHMIST@HOTMAIL.COM

2014

ISBN-13: 978-1502589125
ISBN-10: 1502589125

Preface

This book is based on Programming Problems, by B. R. Green. I was extremely interested and excited when he approached me about writing the `Java` version of the book. `Java`'s popularity and similarity with `C/C++` make it ideal for learning and reviewing algorithms.

Even though I had studied computer science in undergrad, I spent my summers in a research lab rather than interning at different companies. I didn't have any experience with the technical job interview until the year before graduating. As such, I needed to spend more time than most of my peers preparing for job interviews. The interview process was grueling at first, but I got the hang of it over time. Fortunately, I obtained several offers for both software engineering and consulting positions, and I decided to start my tech career in consulting where I obtained a breadth of software experience. I also enjoyed witnessing and participating in both the engineering and business parts of the industry.

Later on I wanted to work on larger scale engineering problems, and so I decided to look for a new opportunity. Having already been through the interview process before, preparing for interviews the second time went faster. After interviewing at a few companies, I decided to go to Facebook for my next adventure.

This book is my attempt at producing the study guide which would have greatly benefited my friends, colleagues, and I when preparing for interviews. It is intended not only for new employees but also seasoned engineers who want a refresher for the technical interview.

Like any profession, interview skills are extremely important. This most definitely applies to the software field as well. Oftentimes I have seen capable candidates who underperform on their interview loop because of their lack of preparation. The algorithms, knowledge, and other skills I learned while preparing for interviews have also been applicable to my job. For example, the process of starting with test cases, brainstorming ideas, and iterating on a solution is a common way of approaching day-to-day work. Having gone through the process of preparing for interviews and having been through multiple interview loops myself, I am also able to do a better job of interviewing other engineers.

Like the original, this book is intended to be a refresher for experienced engineers and a handbook for college students and new candidates. In future editions, the references in this book will be compiled into a bibliography. For the moment, I beg your forgiveness for not knowing where many of the techniques used here were first discovered. I have done my best to ensure the code runs with `Java 1.7` and passes some basic test cases. While the latest stable version of `Java` is `Java 1.8` which was released recently, I specifically chose not to write this book in `Java 1.8` to better illustrate concepts.

0.1 Structure of the book

There are three main areas that I hope to cover in this work: data structures, searching and sorting, and advanced algorithms. The latter section of the text is broken up into algorithms on strings, numbers, and sequences. As the scope of this work grew, it became clear that the work should be divided into two volumes. The first volume provides a discussion of programming problems covering elementary data structures, abstract data types, searching and sorting. The second volume covers advanced programming problems such as spatial partitioning, substring searching, parsing, and sampling.

The chapter structure is the same within both volumes. Each chapter is a mostly self-contained study guide on a specific topic. Where necessary, I've consumed basic algorithms from prior chapters. I attempted to frame it so that complexity increases throughout the chapter. The introductory material should be simply refresher for anyone in the industry; middle sections contain interesting problems and revisions, and the finale an interesting and complex problem. I hope that these problems give the reader some pleasure in thinking about before continuing on to the discussion of the answer.

0.2 Programming in Java

Though not as ubiquitous as C or C++, Java is relatively common in industry. It is not uncommon these days to find undergraduate and graduate school computer science courses taught primarily in Java. Java is an object-oriented language whose syntax is quite similar to that of C and C++. While not the emphasis of this book, some object-oriented concepts will be sprinkled throughout this book - as they are useful concepts every software engineer should be aware of. Given this, I feel this book will be useful even for developers not familiar with or looking to work in a Java environment.

In some places, I have not written well-optimized Java, instead favoring constructs that better portray the concept at hand and are hopefully easier to understand. Where it helps make code cleaner, I have encapsulated broader concepts and data structures within classes and/or helper functions. In general, I have tried to keep the code as readable as possible. I also use Java standard utility functions and classes including arrays, collections, lists, maps, and hashes freely.

0.3 Acknowledgements - B. R. Green

I want to thank L.A.G. for her support and endearing love, and always being there by my side. I also want to thank T.G. for always being there to offer a short diversion to writing, and to my parents R.G. and K.G., for without them I would have never gotten this far.

I also want to thank J. Melvin for a thorough reading, and his helpful comments. The editors of Wikipedia made research extremely efficient, and there is not enough that I can do to thank them for their contribution. And finally, I am grateful to E.M.H. for suggesting this book and her reminder that it should have been completed long ago.

0.4 Acknowledgements - James Wong

I would like to thank my parents, Man W. Wong and Jade Ma, for their love and support throughout all these years. I also want to thank Michael Chong for designing the cover of this book.

Last but not least, I want to thank B. R. Green for mentoring me and giving me the opportunity to write this book with him.

0.5 A last word

In further editions, I hope to make this resemble a proper scientific text. That will require thorough references and proper arguments instead of oblique mentions and assertions of fact. To that end, I am happy to receive your corrections, references, and suggestions regarding any of the material in here at `java.algorithmist@gmail.com` or `algorithmist@hotmail.com`.

Contents

Preface **iii**
0.1 Structure of the book iv
0.2 Programming in Java v
0.3 Acknowledgements - B. R. Green v
0.4 Acknowledgements - James Wong v
0.5 A last word vi

1 The Technical Interview **1**
1.1 An overview 2
1.2 The process 2
1.3 The approach 5

2 Lists **7**
2.1 Definition 7
2.2 Operations 8
2.2.1 Insertion 8
2.2.2 Find 9
2.2.3 Removal 10
2.3 Circular linked-lists 11
2.4 Doubly linked-lists 14
2.5 Selection 16
2.6 Modifications 19
2.7 Multiple lists 20
2.8 Identification 22

3 Trees **27**
3.1 Definition 27
3.2 Operations 28
3.2.1 Insertion 28

3.2.2 Find 29
3.2.3 Removal 30
3.3 Tree properties 33
3.3.1 Size 34
3.3.2 Depth 35
3.3.3 Balance 37
3.3.4 Ancestry 39
3.3.5 Lowest common ancestor 40
3.4 Reconstruction 43
3.4.1 Traversal 43
3.4.2 Reconstructing a tree from a traversal 45

4 Queues and Stacks 47
4.1 Queue 47
4.2 Stack 48
4.3 Implement a queue using a stack 49
4.4 Implement a stack using a queue 52
4.5 Level order traversal 53
4.6 Largest rectangle under a histogram 55

5 Heaps 59
5.1 Definition 59
5.2 Operations 60
5.2.1 Initialization 60
5.2.2 Insertion 62
5.2.3 Find maximum element 63
5.2.4 Remove maximum element 63
5.2.5 Increase key 64
5.3 Enumeration of powers 65
5.4 Find top k elements 68

6 Hash Tables 71
6.1 The hash function 72
6.2 Definition 74
6.3 Operations 77
6.3.1 Insertion 77
6.3.2 Retrieval 77
6.3.3 Dynamic resizing 78
6.4 Collision resolution 79
6.4.1 Separate chaining 79
6.4.2 Open addressing 81

6.4.3 Cuckoo hashing . . . 83
6.5 Find the most common elements in a stream . . . 86
6.6 Implement a most recently used cache . . . 88

7 Binary Search **91**
7.1 Binary search . . . 91
7.2 Find the first occurrence in a sorted array . . . 93
7.3 Search in a rotated array . . . 94
7.4 Find a fixed-point . . . 97
7.5 Find duplicate values . . . 98
7.6 Binary search in a Young Tableau . . . 99

8 Graphical Search **105**
8.1 Definition of a graph . . . 105
8.2 Breadth first search . . . 106
8.2.1 Find the distance between nodes in a graph . 108
8.2.2 Ancestry from genealogical data . . . 110
8.3 Depth first search . . . 112
8.3.1 Determine execution order of a task . . . 113
8.3.2 Find cycles in a graph . . . 115
8.3.3 Find all the words in a boggle game . . . 117
8.4 A^* Search . . . 121

9 Selection **127**
9.1 Selection through sort . . . 128
9.2 The pivot and partition operation . . . 128
9.3 Selection with a pivot . . . 130
9.4 Median of medians . . . 133
9.5 Selection on large data . . . 135

10 Sorting **143**
10.1 Insertion sort . . . 143
10.2 Heap sort . . . 144
10.3 Quick sort . . . 145
10.4 Radix sort . . . 147
10.5 Merge sort . . . 148
10.6 Sorting over large data . . . 150

Afterward **153**

Index **154**

Listings

2.1 Linked-List `Node` 8
2.2 Insert into a Linked-List 9
2.3 Insert into a Sorted Linked-List 9
2.4 Find in a Linked-List 10
2.5 Remove from a Linked-List 11
2.6 Insert into a Circular Linked-List 12
2.7 Find in a Circular Linked-List 13
2.8 Remove from a Circular Linked-List 13
2.9 Doubly Linked-List Node 14
2.10 Insert into a Doubly Linked-List 15
2.11 Find in a Doubly Linked-List 15
2.12 Remove from a Doubly Linked-List 16
2.13 Find the Midpoint of a Linked-List by Counting . . 17
2.14 Find the Midpoint of Linked-List 18
2.15 Find the Node k^{th} from the End 18
2.16 Remove Values from a Linked-List 19
2.17 Reverse a Linked-List 20
2.18 Reverse a Doubly Linked-List 20
2.19 Compare Linked-Lists 21
2.20 Merge Two Linked-Lists 22
2.21 Identify a Doubly Linked-List as a Palindrome . . . 23
2.22 Identify a Linked-List as a Palindrome 24
2.23 Find Loops in a Linked-List 25
3.1 Binary Tree `Node` 28
3.2 Insert into a Binary Search Tree 29
3.3 Find in a Binary Search Tree 30
3.4 Find Parent in a Binary Search Tree 31
3.5 Find Successor in a Binary Search Tree 32
3.6 Remove a Node from a Binary Search Tree 33
3.7 Size of a Binary Tree 34

3.8 Size of a Binary Tree Iterative 35
3.9 Depth of a Binary Tree 36
3.10 Iterative Depth of a Binary Tree 37
3.11 Determine if a Binary Tree is Balanced Naive 38
3.12 Determine if a Binary Tree is Balanced 39
3.13 Find Path from Root to Node 40
3.14 Lowest Common Ancestor from Path to Root 41
3.15 Lowest Common Ancestor Recursive 42
3.16 Lowest Common Ancestor Iterative 43
3.17 In-Order Traversal 44
3.18 Post-Order Traversal 44
3.19 Pre-Order Traversal 45
3.20 Reconstruction of a Binary Tree 46
4.1 Queue Class 48
4.2 Stack Class 49
4.3 Implement Queue from a Stack 51
4.4 Implement Stack from a Queue 53
4.5 Level Order Traversal 54
4.6 Level Order Traversal with Separation Tokens 55
4.7 Definition of `Histogram` 56
4.8 Largest Rectangle Under Histogram 57
5.1 Heap Index of Children 61
5.2 Heap Index of Parent 61
5.3 Heap Creation 62
5.4 Insert Into a Heap 63
5.5 Find Maximum in a Heap 63
5.6 Remove Maximum from a Heap 64
5.7 Increase a Key in a Heap 65
5.8 ValueTerm Pair 66
5.9 Enumeration of Powers 67
5.10 Find Max Value in an Array 68
5.11 Find Top k Elements of a Stream 69
6.1 A Simple Hash Function 73
6.2 Another Hash Function 73
6.3 Complex Hash Table 74
6.4 Definition of `Item` object 75
6.5 Definition of Hashtable 75
6.6 Simple Hashtable 76
6.7 Insert into a Hashtable 77
6.8 Find in a Hashtable 78
6.9 Dynamic Resizing of a Hashtable 78

6.10 Definition of Hashtable with Separate Chaining . . . 80
6.11 Insert with Separate Chaining 80
6.12 Find with Separate Chaining 81
6.13 Insert with Open Addressing 82
6.14 Find with Open Addressing 83
6.15 Definition of Hashtable with Cuckoo Hashing 84
6.16 Insert with Cuckoo Hashing 85
6.17 Find with Cuckoo Hashing 86
6.18 Find the Most Common Element 87
6.19 Most Recently Used Cache 88
6.20 Retrieval in Most Recently Used Cache 89
6.21 Access Recording in Most Recently Used Cache . . . 89
7.1 Binary Search 92
7.2 Binary Search to Find Leftmost Target 93
7.3 Binary Search in Rotated Array 95
7.4 Binary Search with Pivot Offset 96
7.5 Binary Search for the Pivot in Rotated Array 97
7.6 Find a Fixed-Point 98
7.7 Find Duplicates in a Sequence 99
7.8 Definition of a Coordinate 100
7.9 Definition of a Matrix 100
7.10 Diagonal Search of a Matrix 101
7.11 Find Lower Bound 102
7.12 Binary Search in Young Tableau 103
8.1 Graph `Node` 106
8.2 Visitor Interface 107
8.3 Breadth First Search 107
8.4 Shortest Path Distances 109
8.5 Ancestry from Genealogical Data 111
8.6 Decide if Two People are Related 111
8.7 Depth First Search 113
8.8 Dependency graph 114
8.9 Detect Cycles 116
8.10 Definition of a Boggle Board 117
8.11 Definition of a Position on the Board 118
8.12 Word Search in a Matrix from a Single Point 120
8.13 Word Search in a Matrix 121
8.14 Admissible Maze Distance Heuristic 122
8.15 Definition of `DistancePosition` 122
8.16 Search Through a Maze 124
9.1 Selection by Sorting 128

9.2 Median by Sorting 128
9.3 Partition on an Element 130
9.4 Definition of Find Pivot Index 131
9.5 Selection with Pivot 132
9.6 Median of 3 133
9.7 Median of Medians 134
9.8 Definition of `ArrayBounds` in Selection on Large Data 136
9.9 Initialization for Selection on Large Data 136
9.10 Definition of `Pivot` in Selection on Large Data . . . 137
9.11 Find the nth Element in an Array 138
9.12 Median of Large Data 139
9.13 Partition an Array Around a Given Value 140
9.14 Partition Array on Pivot 141
9.15 Update Search Bounds After Partition 142
10.1 Insertion Sort 144
10.2 Heap Sort 145
10.3 Quick Sort 146
10.4 Radix Sort 147
10.5 Merge Sort 149
10.6 Sorting Large Data with Merge Sort 151

Chapter 1

The Technical Interview

For both sides of an interview there is an art. The art is at its best when, at the end of an hour, both parties leave the interview feeling they have spent a productive hour. For the interviewer, it is asking a challenging but tractable question and working with the candidate to find an optimal solution. It is making the candidate feel welcome, valued, and excited to be offered an opportunity to work alongside others who have a passion for technology. And it is being comfortable in the decision to give the candidate a hire or no hire decision.

But of course the candidate has a more complicated role. Even so it is simple to state what must be done; one must be friendly, be straightforward, and know your fundamentals. There is not much else you can do to prepare for an interview.

The main purpose of this book is to provide a refresher for the fundamentals of programming that come up in technical interviews. We do this by presenting interview questions that have been asked in the field, and answering them in as much completeness as will be required by any technical interview. We strive to provide a number of solutions to each question, in order that the reader can understand the difference between a bad and good solution.

1.1 An overview

There is no secret recipe to acing an interview or solving a programming problem. And even if you know your foundations, in the course of a tech career everyone will come across that interviewer who is annoyed at having to interview, suffering from an inferiority complex, or just plain determined to give you a no hire. But there are a number of things you can do to increase your odds of getting a hire.

First, know what you are getting into. If you have never interviewed before, then the section on the technical interview loop is the place to familiarize yourself with what will be happening.

Second, turn the interview into a conversation. Take turns speaking, ask real questions, and overall be honest. Honesty will make the discussion easier and more enjoyable for both sides. Of course in any technical interview you will be required to present a solution to a coding question, but that will only be about half the time. You can gauge your success by how long the interviewer allows the conversation to run over.

Third, approach the technical question systematically and answer it completely. And, this is very important, do it right the first time.

1.2 The process

In tech, the fundamental unit of hiring is the technical interview. In general, the technical interview is a 45-minute to one hour one-on-one session in which an interviewer asks a candidate to solve one or more programming questions

While screenings and introductions may be handled by human resource personnel, software engineers always conduct technical interviews. These engineers may be individual contributors or managers, but they are always active in the field and are active on a project. Interviewing is not a specialty of software engineering, so most of the interviewers any candidate will see are volunteers from different groups or areas within a company. The exception is the hiring manager, if the loop has one. While they are all volunteers, these interviewers are trained to respect hiring law and avoid certain questions that the company has found useless or harmful. But beyond those small exceptions, all have the freedom to ask any technical question they desire.

Every interviewer has a set of technical questions they prefer. These have been gathered from his or her past interviews, come from current or past project, or has been cultivated by lunchroom discussions with fellow employees. The last part is important to the process. While generally there is a central organization training interviewers, every company has an interview culture where questions are shared and analyzed in an open discussion. And this culture does well to keep the questions in check more than any centralized training.

The point of the technical interview is for the interviewer to gather as much signal from the candidate as possible in order to answer the question "Does this candidate meet the bar." The bar refers to the standard for hiring of the company. Every company has a similar standard with minor variations. They answer the question in relation to the company, the group, or the individual. For Google, they are looking for someone who is at least as good as the average Googler. For Microsoft, they are looking for someone who is smart and at least as good as the average person in the product group. For Facebook, they are looking for someone who is better than the interviewer. Even so, each interviewer's standards vary as well. But the bottom line is that a candidate will pass the bar if the interviewer wants to work with the candidate. Passing the bar is met with a decision of hire, and the decision of no hire is given otherwise.

Technical interviews have a progression. At one end is the initial screening. The initial screen is done on the phone, video chat, and only rarely in person. The initial screening is always a series of simple, straightforward questions. The programming component may include questions such as writing `atoi`, binary search, or reversing a linked list. The purpose of the initial screening is to try to not waste employees' time if the candidate is clearly below the bar. There are three things the interviewer is looking for in the initial screening: can the candidate write a simple program, can the candidate communicate effectively, and is the candidate being slotted for the right job. The last question is usually one of technical versus managerial or back-end versus front-end specialties.

After the initial screen is the on-site loop. The interview loop is a series of four or more technical interviews with the goal to see if a consensus on hiring can be made. The loop is conducted onsite, either at a company's main campus or remote interviewing session.

This daylong gauntlet is generally the final hurdle to a hire or no hire decision by the company.

The loop is designed to ask a sequence of moderately difficult questions to measure a candidate's competency, creativity, and cultural fit. A normal mix of questions involves two programming questions, a design question, and an algorithms question. Programming questions are the heart of the technical interview, and a candidate will generally see more of these than less.

The implementation of the loop differs only slightly from company to company.

At Microsoft, interviewers shuffle a candidate between their offices. During this transition they will share initial feedback immediately in order to shift focus during the day. For instance if a candidate has shown great mastery in algorithms, an interviewer may suggest focusing on design. If a candidate fumbles a question in design, an interviewer may suggest that a follow-up is made.

The process is different at Google and new companies. Since these companies do not provide their employees offices, a candidate is assigned to a meeting room and interviewers come to him or her throughout the day. Also at Google and new companies, interviewers have little to no contact with each other throughout the entire process other than to avoid question duplication. At Google, questions are written down on a sheet of paper that is shuffled between interviewers. While this may give the candidate a feeling of disjointed disorganization, it is done to attempt to eliminate bias from other interviewers' decisions.

At the end of the technical interview, feedback is collated into a hiring packet and a decision is made. At Microsoft, the hiring manager often makes the decision the same day and a candidate can expect a phone call with an offer within a week. At Google and Facebook, the feedback is made by a local hiring committee and forwarded to a final hiring committee. The committee is a sanity check on the interviewer's consensus aimed at maintaining a high hiring bar. The cost of this process is that it may be many weeks after the loop before a candidate gets an offer or no hire decision.

Keep in mind that a single no hire during a loop is usually not enough to stop the process. However, a sequence of no hires and very weak hires, or a continued failure to answer basic questions definitely is enough. What the hiring manager or hiring committee is looking for is confidence from the interviewers in their decisions, a breadth of knowledge demonstrated by the candidate, good communication skills, and an answer to the question "Does the candidate meet our bar?"

1.3 The approach

A good interview question has many right answers but always at least one optimal in time or space. Getting to the optimal solution will take mastery of the fundamentals: data structure, memory management, iteration style, and search techniques.

It is important that you know how to approach technical questions. Every candidate should learn to take his time in order to consider all these angles. Take your time. After all if an interviewer asks you to code up lowest common ancestor in a binary search tree and you approach it for an unstructured binary tree you have made an error that will cost you a hire.

There is a simple, natural approach to problem solving that I see all well-prepared candidates take. The steps are restating the question, understanding what is required, sketching a solution, coding, and testing. Let's go through each of these steps in turn.

First restate the problem. You should look for ambiguity, and if found continue by either proposing changes or asking for clarification. Ambiguity comes in many forms, so be on the lookout for undefined behavior and corner cases.

Second, make sure you understand the corner cases and you've defined away as much ambiguity as possible. Do a few test cases with the interviewer. Write down the input and expected output, and leave these on the board to refer back to later. These cases will be useful during sketching and testing.

Third, sketch the program on the board. Do not take the whole board, because you will need to write the code next. But you want to have something to refer back to while you present your solution. Your sketch should be enough to show what you'll need to write for your main processing path and what helper functions you'll need to write. Your sketch should also be complete enough to gauge the asymptotic run time of your algorithm.

Fourth, write the program correctly. It cannot be said enough - you are best off to do it right the first time. Many candidates ask if they can skip error checking, boundary conditions, or helper functions that they believe are not core to the problem at hand. Do not do this. To see why simply compare two candidates, one in which after writing the prototype the candidate automatically begins checking for `null` and buffer length, and another in which the candidate waves his hand and says that he will do normal error and bounds checking later. All else being equal, the first candidate is the better interview. And that is because he showed he could do it right the first time.

Fifth and lastly, run your test cases from the second step through the code you wrote on the board. This gives you a chance to show the interviewer how you test, and also lets you see you own writing with fresh eyes. Perhaps you changed a variable name, missed a boundary case, or improperly changed a helper function prototype. By stepping through your test cases these problems will be avoided. And that is it. Restate the problem, write down some test cases, sketch you approach, write the program, and test it. This should sound familiar, because it's no coincidence that interviewing and every day programming have the same workflow.

Working through programming problems is much more enjoyable than talking about strategies on how to approach them, so let's begin. First up is a review of the fundamentals of programming.

Chapter 2

Lists

We begin our reference section on data types with the linked-list.

A linked-list is a basic data structure often used as the underlying data type of other structures such as stacks and queues. Linked-lists benefit from constant time insertion and removal, but come at the cost of linear time search. This is because linked-lists do not support random access; hence, search and removal require a full scan of the linked-list.

Common programming problems for lists are often exercises in identifying boundary cases, clever traversal techniques, and judicious use of temporary variables. In this section we will implement a linked-list and its operations, and then solve many of the basic questions about linked-lists.

2.1 Definition

A linked-list is a structure composed of list nodes. A list node contains some data for the node, as well as a reference to the next node in the list. In the following sections, we will use the definition below for a node.

Listing 2.1: Linked-List Node

```
class Node {
  Node next;
  int data;

  Node(int data) {
    this(null, data);
  }

  Node(Node head, int data) {
    this.next = head;
    this.data = data;
  }
}
```

The first node, referred to as the head, identifies the list. A reference to the head is enough to identify the entire list. Empty lists are identified as those whose head is null.

2.2 Operations

The basic operations of a linked-list are insert, find, and remove. More complex operations can be built up from these operations. In the next section we implement each of the basic operations.

2.2.1 Insertion

Insertion in a linked-list is constant time because the data type supports only a push-front operation. That is the current head of the list is replaced with a new node with the specified value. There are two special cases for insertion, inserting into an empty list and inserting into the head of a list. However, with a complete listing of the constructors of the data structure, this complexity is easily removed at the cost of requiring an update to head with the result of the insertion.

Listing 2.2: Insert into a Linked-List

```
Node insert(Node head, int data) {
  return new Node(head, data);
}
```

Interviews often ask for insertion into a sorted list. A clever question for a candidate to ask is whether or not a list was the right choice for a container if the data needs to remain sorted. But for answering this question, the boundary cases are inserting into the head or tail of the list. To insert into a sorted linked-list, we look for the predecessor of where the data should be inserted. When found, we construct a new node, and splice it into the list by updating the proper `next` member variables.

Listing 2.3: Insert into a Sorted Linked-List

```
Node insert_sorted(Node head, int data) {
  if (head == null || data <= head.data) {
    return new Node(head, data);
  }
  Node current = head;
  while (null != current.next
         && current.next.data < data) {
    current = current.next;
  }
  if (null == current.next) {
    current.next = new Node(data);
  } else {
    current.next = new Node(current.next, data);
  }
  return head;
}
```

2.2.2 Find

Because random access is not supported, the only traversal supported considers each node in turn. Hence search in a linked-list is a linear time operation. As such, when retrieving a node of a linked-list by key, we must scan until a target has been located or every node has been considered. This is implemented in the `find` operation.

Listing 2.4: Find in a Linked-List

```
Node find(Node head, int value) {
  while (null != head && head.data != value) {
    head = head.next;
  }
  return head;
}
```

2.2.3 Removal

Removal of data from a linked-list takes a reference to a node as an identifier. The boundary cases are removal of the head or tail, and deletion from a single-item list. Removal of the head requires special care, because lists are identified by their head element. If that is removed, then the head needs to be updated. A simpler method is to copy data of the successor into the head and remove the successor. However this trick requires special casing the single item list. As above, we require special handling for the head after calling remove. Removal from the tail requires maintenance of the tail predecessor.

Listing 2.5: Remove from a Linked-List

```
Node remove(Node head, Node target) {
  while (head != null && head == target) {
    head = head.next;
  }
  if (null == head) {
    return null;
  }
  Node current = head;
  while (null != current.next) {
    if (current.next == target) {
      current.next = current.next.next;
    }
    current = current.next;
  }
  return head;
}
```

Note that as the target of removal was a parameter, we can assume that it was not `null` and the list was not empty. For this reason we did not verify that the head of the list was not `null`. We will follow this pattern in the subsequent examples as well.

2.3 Circular linked-lists

A common modification to linked-lists is called a circular linked-list. The structure defining a node in a circular linked-list is identical to that of a node in a simple linked-list. However, the update and remove rules are modified to maintain that the tail of the list points back to the head.

Insertion into a circular linked-list is similar to that in a standard list except the head element must reference itself in a list of length 1. We also lose the idea of simply replacing the head with a new reference, since the tail refers to the head.

Listing 2.6: Insert into a Circular Linked-List

```
Node circular_insert(Node head, int data) {
  Node insertion = new Node(data);
  if (null == head) {
    insertion.next = insertion;
    return insertion;
  }
  if (head.data == head.next.data) {
    head.next = insertion;
    insertion.next = head;
    return insertion;
  }
  int headData = head.data;
  insertion.data = headData;
  head.data = data;
  insertion.next = head.next;
  head.next = insertion;
  return head;
}
```

Retrieval in a circular linked-list is almost as simple as that in a simple linked-list. Again, the entire list must be enumerated until the value has been found or every node has been visited. Unlike in a simple linked-list, termination of the search cannot rely on finding `null`. Instead we must cache a reference to the head and use it to determine when the list has looped back.

Listing 2.7: Find in a Circular Linked-List

```
Node circular_find(Node head, int value) {
  Node current = head;
  while (null != current
         && current.data != value) {
    current = current.next;
    if (current.data == head.data) {
      return null;
    }
  }
  return current;
}
```

Removal from a circular linked-list is more complex than removal in a simple linked-list. As with insertion, this is because the tail element refers to the head element. To get around this, we do not remove the desired node, but instead shift all the elements of a list around it. This avoids the problems of updating the value of the predecessor's `next` member variable.

Removal also requires checking the boundary case where there is but a single element in the circular linked-list. Then we must clear the list entirely.

Listing 2.8: Remove from a Circular Linked-List

```
Node circular_remove(Node head, Node target) {
  if (null == head
      || (head == target && head.next == target)) {
    return null;
  }
  Node next = target.next;
  target.data = next.data;
  target.next = next.next;
  return target;
}
```

2.4 Doubly linked-lists

Doubly linked-lists are lists in which each node has both a reference to the next element in the list as well as the previous element in the list. A simple doubly linked-list has a head with `null` as its `prev` member, and a tail with `null` as its `next` member. Doubly linked-lists can also be circular, with single element lists having both the head and tail referencing the same node. In the following examples we implement circular doubly linked-lists.

The constructor for a doubly linked-list is only a simple modification of a simple linked-list `Node` where a `prev` member variable is added.

Listing 2.9: Doubly Linked-List Node

```
class DllNode {
  DllNode prev;
  DllNode next;
  int data;

  DllNode(int data) {
    this(null, null, data);
  }

  DllNode(DllNode prev, DllNode next, int data) {
    this.prev = prev == null ? this : prev;
    this.next = next == null ? this : next;
    this.data = data;
  }
}
```

Inserting and removing from a circular doubly linked-list integrates inserting into a standard linked-list and the semantics of a circular linked-list. The implementation below pushes the list forward and inserts a new head. This is done by first setting the `next` and `prev` members appropriately, and then correcting the list structure before returning.

Listing 2.10: Insert into a Doubly Linked-List

```
DllNode insert(DllNode head, int data) {
  if (null == head) {
    return new DllNode(data);
  }
  DllNode insertion =
    new DllNode(head.prev, head, data);
  insertion.prev.next = insertion;
  insertion.next.prev = insertion;
  return insertion;
}
```

The find operation for a doubly linked-list is identical to that of the find operation for a circular linked-list, aside from the parameter and return type. The previous code will operate on doubly linked-lists with only that modifcation.

Listing 2.11: Find in a Doubly Linked-List

```
DllNode find(DllNode head, int value) {
  DllNode current = head;
  while (null != current
         && current.data != value) {
    current = current.next;
    if (current.data == head.data) {
      return null;
    }
  }
  return current;
}
```

Removal from a circular doubly linked-list is simpler than that of a simple linked-list. This is because each node of doubly linked-list has a reference to its previous element. This makes splicing a node out of a doubly linked-list trivial, where in a simple linked-list we needed to remove the next node and swap data values.

Listing 2.12: Remove from a Doubly Linked-List

```
DllNode remove(DllNode head, DllNode target) {
  if (head != null
      && head.next == head
      && head  == target) {
    return null;
  }
  target.prev.next = target.next;
  target.next.prev = target.prev;
  if (head == target) {
    head = target.next;
  }
  return head;
}
```

2.5 Selection

Since a linked-list is unordered and does not support random access, the question of finding the value at interesting positions within the list requires clever solutions. These are called selection problems. To being, consider finding the middle element of a linked-list. A straightforward method is to count the number of elements and then scan for the element at that index.

Listing 2.13: Find the Midpoint of a Linked-List by Counting

```
Node mid_by_counting(Node head) {
  if (null == head) {
    return head;
  }
  Node trailing = head;
  int size = 0;
  while (null != head) {
    size++;
    head = head.next;
  }
  int mid = size / 2;
  while (mid-- != 0) {
    trailing = trailing.next;
  }
  return trailing;
}
```

This operation obviously requires one and a half full scans of the list. But we can do better. Consider what happens when we move two indices through the list in tandem. Concretely, we move one index a single node at a time and another two nodes at a time. When the first index is at node x, the second reference is at position $2x$. So when the second node reaches the end of the list the first reference is at the midpoint! So indeed, we can do this with a single scan.

Listing 2.14: Find the Midpoint of Linked-List

```
Node mid(Node head) {
  Node trailing = head;
  while (null != head) {
    head = head.next;
    if (null != head) {
      head = head.next;
      trailing = trailing.next;
    }
  }
  return trailing;
}
```

This trick can be generalized to find any element at some fraction of the length of the list. So for any k we can find the element at position $length/k$. But often the question is finding the element at the fixed position k from the end. We can find the node at position k from the end of the list by modifying the trick above in that we move two references in tandem, but give one a head start.

Listing 2.15: Find the Node k^{th} from the End

```
Node kth_from_end(Node head, int k) {
  Node trailing = head;
  while (k-- > 0 && null != head) {
    head = head.next;
  }
  while (null != head && null != head.next) {
    head = head.next;
    trailing = trailing.next;
  }
  return trailing;
}
```

2.6 Modifications

Along with selection, lack of random access gives rise to a number of problems that ask for modifications of a list. The most basic is the removal of all nodes matching a certain value. The only modification required of the `remove` method is to maintain the current scan position in order to continue iterating after a node has been removed. Maintaining a trailing reference and removing leading nodes that match the value can accomplish this. In this approach, care must be taken to remove all leading nodes that match, else successive matches will not be handled correctly. In the implementation, successive matches are handled by the inner `while` loop in the listing below.

Listing 2.16: Remove Values from a Linked-List

```
Node remove_values(Node head, int value) {
  while (head != null && head.data == value) {
    head = head.next;
  }
  if (null == head) {
    return null;
  }
  Node current = head;
  while (null != current.next) {
    if (current.next.data == value) {
      current.next = current.next.next;
    }
    current = current.next;
  }
  return head;
}
```

Only a bit more complex is the issue of reversing the order of the nodes in a linked-list. In a linked-list, this can be done without constructing a new list by maintaining the current scan position while simultaneously modifying the node previously scanned. As the algorithm iterates over the list, it is reversing the successor-predecessor relationships. After full iteration, the list is reversed.

Listing 2.17: Reverse a Linked-List

```
Node reverse(Node head) {
  Node prev = null;
  while (null != head) {
    Node temp = head.next;
    head.next = prev;
    prev = head;
    head = temp;
  }
  return prev;
}
```

Reversing a circular doubly linked-list can be done with the same technique. However as is usual with circular linked-lists we must keep track of the terminal condition.

Listing 2.18: Reverse a Doubly Linked-List

```
DllNode reverse(DllNode head) {
  if (null == head) {
    return null;
  }
  if (head.next == head.prev) {
    return head;
  }
  DllNode tail = head;
  do {
    DllNode temp = tail.next;
    tail.next = tail.prev;
    tail.prev = temp;
    tail = temp;
  } while (tail.data != head.data);
  return head.next;
}
```

2.7 Multiple lists

Many problems require working with multiple lists simultaneously.

Above, we saw how we can find the midpoint of a list by moving two references in tandem. Using the same idea we can solve the problem of comparing two lists with a single pass over each. Comparison is only difficult in that there is no random access. We use multiple references, one for each list in question.

We first check that both lists are either empty or not empty. Afterward, we take it in turns to compare each element.

Listing 2.19: Compare Linked-Lists

```
boolean equals(Node x, Node y) {
  while (null != x && null != y) {
    if (x.data != y.data) {
      return false;
    }
    x = x.next;
    y = y.next;
  }
  return null == x && null == y;
}
```

The listing above compares two lists, but can easily be generalized to compare an arbitrary number simultaneously.

The other common operation on multiple linked-lists is merging, in which two or more lists become one. Since linked-lists are dynamically bound, merging two linked-lists can be done without the allocation of any new memory. A naive method to merge is to append one list to another by iteratively walking one list and inserting each node into the other. This method requires as many writes as there are elements in the list.

We can do better. We need only append one list to another, as in the listing below. Appending in this manner is a single write operation, although one list must be read to the end.

Listing 2.20: Merge Two Linked-Lists

```
Node merge(Node h1, Node h2) {
  if (null == h1 || null == h2) {
    return (null != h1) ? h1 : h2;
  }
  Node head = h1;
  while (null != h1.next) {
    h1 = h1.next;
  }
  h1.next = h2;
  return head;
}
```

2.8 Identification

The final set of problems for linked-lists involves the identification of list properties. Below we consider two problems: determining whether or not a list is a palindrome, and determining if it has self-loops.

A palindrome is a sequence that is the same both forward and backward. Deciding if a linked-list is a palindrome is an exercise in combining state information and selection. At first glance, one can be perplexed how to efficiently compare the first and last nodes, the second and second from last nodes, et cetera until the midpoint. Let's first consider this question with a doubly linked-list. In this case we have forward and backward enumeration, and a solution is easily found. We iterate forward and backward until the two iterators cross.

Listing 2.21: Identify a Doubly Linked-List as a Palindrome

```
boolean is_palindrome(DllNode head) {
  if (null == head
      || head.data == head.next.data) {
    return true;
  }
  DllNode tail = head.prev;
  do {
    if (head.data != tail.data) {
      return false;
    }
    head = head.next;
    tail = tail.prev;
  } while (head.data != tail.data
          && head.data != tail.next.data);
  return true;
}
```

Returning to a simple linked-list, we found ourselves without a reverse iterator. But a single scan with extra memory makes this simpler. We can put the nodes in a stack, and then inspect the list back to front. This allows us to iterate in reverse as we unroll the stack.

Listing 2.22: Identify a Linked-List as a Palindrome

```
boolean is_palindrome(Node head) {
  Node temp = head;
  Stack<Node> s = new Stack<Node>();
  while (null != temp) {
    s.push(temp);
    temp = temp.next;
  }
  while (!s.empty()) {
    if (head.data != s.peek().data) {
      return false;
    }
    s.pop();
    head = head.next;
  }
  return true;
}
```

The most famous interview question regarding lists is the identification of self-loops in a list. On first thought, the idea is simply to collect the nodes until we find two that are identical. Often a candidate will jump on the hash table solution. The reason is hash tables have constant time access, and collision detection is a basic problem in that data type. If any collisions are found, the first one is guaranteed to be the head of the loop. However, since the question was posed as a decision problem, we are doing too much work. This solution requires the allocation of new memory at least as large as the number of nodes in the list. A better option is a modification of our solution to the selection problem.

Consider what happens when we try to find the midpoint of a circularly linked-list. Instead of terminating, eventually the lead reference will catch up to the tail reference. So if ever the lead and trailing references coincide, we know there is a loop. But if the lead reference finds the terminating `null`, then we know there is no loop. We can turn this insight into a solution to the problem of identifying self-loops in a linked-list.

Listing 2.23: Find Loops in a Linked-List

```
boolean detect_loop(Node head) {
  if (null == head) {
    return false;
  }
  Node trailing = head;
  Node leading = head;
  while (null != leading) {
    leading = leading.next;
    if (trailing == leading) {
      return true;
    }
    trailing = trailing.next;
    if (null != leading) {
      leading = leading.next;
    }
  }
  return false;
}
```

This solves the problem without needing to allocate extra memory and with the added cost savings of not having to compute a hash value, resolve hash collisions, or dynamically resize a hash table. The elegance of this solution is the reason it has been asked as a Microsoft interview question for nearly 30 years.

Chapter 3

Trees

We continue our review of data types with a discussion on binary search trees.

As a data structure, the binary tree overcomes the inefficiencies of retrieval in a linked-list. However, the logarithmic running time for retrieval comes at the cost of increasing the time for insertion and deletion from constant to logarithmic time. Algorithms for binary tree operations are also more complex to write than the analogous algorithms for linked-lists. For instance, for operations where a linked-list used iteration, the operation on a binary tree may rely upon recursion. In this section we will review the basic operations on binary search trees, and begin to solve more complex interview questions.

3.1 Definition

A binary tree is composed of tree nodes. Tree nodes consist of a data member variable and the address of two other nodes. These other nodes are called children, and are distinguished as *left* and *right*.

Listing 3.1: Binary Tree Node

```
class Node {
  int value;
  Node left;
  Node right;

  Node(int value) {
    this.value = value;
  }
}
```

As was the case with a linked-list, a binary tree is a referred to by a reference to a designated node. This node is called the *root*. Empty trees are those whose root is `null`.

A binary search tree is a binary tree that maintains a sort order between the parent and children nodes. The order invariant is whenever a node has a left or right child, `node.value > left.value` and `node.value <= right.value`. A binary search tree is balanced when for every node, the depth of the sub-trees from the left child and right child differ by at most one. Most of the complexity bounds discussed below hold only for balanced binary search trees

In this section, we will focus our attention on operations and algorithms concerning a binary search trees. We further assume that the binary search trees are balanced. Finally, as before we assume that the tree operations below are responsible for memory management but the caller is responsible for updating the root.

3.2 Operations

The basic operations of a binary search tree are `insert`, `find`, and `remove`. In the following we will also look at the operations of `find_parent` and `find_successor`, as we will see that they are necessary precursors for node removal.

3.2.1 Insertion

Insertion in a binary search tree is a logarithmic time operation. This is because to maintain the order invariant, an insertion requires search to identify which node in a tree will become the parent of the inserted node. After a parent node is identified by a find operation, only a constant number of operations are needed to complete insertion.

Listing 3.2: Insert into a Binary Search Tree

```
Node insert(Node root, int val) {
  if (null == root) {
    return new Node(val);
  }
  if (val < root.value) {
    root.left = insert(root.left, val);
  } else {
    root.right = insert(root.right, val);
  }
  return root;
}
```

Also notice the use of recursion during the retrieval phase of insertion which is characteristic of binary search trees. Whereas algorithms on linked-lists are usually iterative, operations on trees are often recursive.

3.2.2 Find

The utility of a binary search tree is derived from the logarithmic time search guarantee of the data structure. This guarantee is only for balanced binary search trees. Search is the motivation for use of a binary tree, and as such is the fundamental operation on binary search trees.

Listing 3.3: Find in a Binary Search Tree

```
Node find(Node root, int val) {
  if (null == root || root.value == val) {
    return root;
  }
  if (val < root.value) {
    return find(root.left, val);
  }
  return find(root.right, val);
}
```

Note that the logarithmic time for search is guaranteed because when we branch left or right, we are decreasing the search space by a constant fraction. Each branch cuts the search space in half. We can only divide the search space by two a logarithmic number of times before we are left with a single element.

3.2.3 Removal

As with insertion, removal of a value from a binary search tree has logarithmic running time. The search is required for more than the care needed to maintain the order invariant. Indeed, search is required to find the next value in the binary search tree that is compatible with the position of the node being removed. When this is found, that value is replaced and the node found is removed.

In order to carefully write the algorithm for removal, we will first define two ancillary functions `find_parent` and `find_successor`. Finding the parent of a node is a straightforward operation. It is simply a modified find operation in which the parent node is returned, not the child. The solution below returns `null` if the node is the root.

Listing 3.4: Find Parent in a Binary Search Tree

```
Node find_parent(Node root, Node target) {
  if (root == target) {
    return null;
  }
  while (root.left != target
         && root.right != target) {
    if (target.value < root.value) {
      root = root.left;
    } else {
      root = root.right;
    }
  }
  return root;
}
```

The find parent operation is used to find the successor of a node in a binary search tree. Every node in binary search tree has a data member with a comparison operation. Suppose the data in a binary tree is sorted in increasing order. The successor of a target node is a node in a binary search binary tree whose data would immediately follow the target node's data in a sorted list of all the data members associated with the binary tree. The successor plays a role in removal from a binary search tree in that it can replace the target node and maintain the order invariant.

Listing 3.5: Find Successor in a Binary Search Tree

```
Node find_successor(Node root, Node target) {
  Node successor = target.right;
  if (null != successor) {
    while (null != successor.left) {
      successor = successor.left;
    }
    return successor;
  }
  do {
    if (null != successor) {
      target = successor;
    }
    successor = find_parent(root, target);
  } while (null != successor
          && successor.right == target);
  return successor;
}
```

Removal from a binary search tree has a number of cases that need to be considered to maintain the order invariant. Removing a leaf node is simple, since the node has no children it can be deallocated and the parent updated. If a node has a single child, then that child can replace the node in the binary search tree and the node deallocated. In the final case when a node has two children, we want to replace the node with the value of its successor. Doing so would maintain the order invariant at the node's location in a binary search tree. We then need to recursively remove the successor from the tree to avoid having a duplicate node. Altogether, this provides the following algorithm.

Listing 3.6: Remove a Node from a Binary Search Tree

```
Node remove(Node root, Node target) {
  if (null != target.left
      && null != target.right) {
    Node next = find_successor(root, target);
    int data = next.value;
    remove(root, next);
    target.value = data;
    return root;
  }
  if (null != target.left
      || null != target.right) {
    Node temp = (null != target.left)
      ? target.left
      : target.right;
    target.value = temp.value;
    target.left = temp.left;
    target.right = temp.right;
    return root;
  }
  if (root == target) {
    return null;
  }
  Node parent = find_parent(root, target);
  if (parent.left == target) {
    parent.left = null;
  } else {
    parent.right = null;
  }
  return root;
}
```

3.3 Tree properties

Tree algorithms rely on many properties of a tree. For instance a tree's size, depth and whether or not it is balanced. Below we provide algorithms for calculating commonly asked properties of a binary tree.

3.3.1 Size

The size of a binary tree is its number of nodes. Notice that from any node, the size of the sub-tree rooted at that node is one more than the sum of the size of the sub-trees rooted at its children. We can easily calculate the size of a binary tree recursively.

Listing 3.7: Size of a Binary Tree

```
int size(Node root) {
  if (null == root) {
    return 0;
  }
  return 1 + size(root.left) + size(root.right);
}
```

As an exercise, consider how to calculate the size of a binary tree without recursion. In this alternative we can count the number of nodes while iterating through the tree.

Listing 3.8: Size of a Binary Tree Iterative

```
int size_iterative(Node root) {
  if (null == root) {
    return 0;
  }
  int count = 0;
  Queue<Node> q = new LinkedList<Node>();
  q.add(root);
  while (!q.isEmpty()) {
    Node front = q.poll();
    count++;
    if (null != front.left) {
      q.add(front.left);
    }
    if (null != front.right) {
      q.add(front.right);
    }
  }
  return count;
}
```

The traversal used above is called a breadth first. We will examine it in a more general setting later.

3.3.2 Depth

The depth of a binary tree is the length of the longest simple path from the root to a leaf node. The depth from a node is one more than the depth of that node's deepest sub-tree, so there is an immediate recursive solution.

Listing 3.9: Depth of a Binary Tree

```
int depth(Node root) {
  if (null == root) {
    return 0;
  }
  return 1 + Math.max(depth(root.left),
                      depth(root.right));
}
```

Let's consider an iterative solution. We will again traverse the tree, but this time repeatedly to the leaf nodes. In order to determine if we are branching left or right in a depth first enumeration, we keep track of the list of visited nodes in a set. At any point in the algorithm below, the stack contains the path from the root to the node on top of the stack, so the current depth is equal to the size of the stack. The max depth of any leaf is equal to the depth of the binary search tree.

Listing 3.10: Iterative Depth of a Binary Tree

```
int depth_iterative(Node root) {
  if (null == root) {
    return 0;
  }
  int max_depth = 0;
  Set<Node> visited = new HashSet<Node>();
  Stack<Node> s = new Stack<Node>();
  s.push(root);
  while (!s.isEmpty()) {
    Node top = s.peek();
    if (null != top.left
        && !visited.contains(top.left)) {
      s.push(top.left);
    } else if (null != top.right
               && !visited.contains(top.right)) {
      s.push(top.right);
    } else {
      visited.add(top);
      max_depth = Math.max(max_depth, s.size());
      s.pop();
    }
  }
  return max_depth;
}
```

The traversal used above is called a depth first traversal. As with the breadth first traversal, we will examine it in a more general setting later.

3.3.3 Balance

A binary tree is balanced if for every node the difference between the depth of its left and right sub-trees is at most one. To determine whether or not a binary tree is balanced we must evaluate whether or not every sub-tree is balanced. Doing so naively would require multiple calculations of depth.

Listing 3.11: Determine if a Binary Tree is Balanced Naive

```
boolean balanced_naive(Node root) {
  if (null == root) {
    return true;
  }
  if (!balanced(root.left)
      || !balanced(root.right)) {
    return false;
  }
  int left_depth = depth(root.left);
  int right_depth = depth(root.right);
  return Math.abs(right_depth - left_depth) <= 1;
}
```

However, this solution is wasteful. We are repeatedly recalculating the depth, and in an unbalanced tree this is a quadratic solution.

A linear solution would require modifying the recursion to return the depth of the sub-tree as well as if it is balanced or not. The run time gains come from reusing the partial calculations made in determining if the left and right sub-trees are balanced.

Listing 3.12: Determine if a Binary Tree is Balanced

```
boolean balanced_depth(Node root, int[] depth) {
  if (null == root) {
    depth[0] = 0;
    return true;
  }
  int[] left = new int[1];
  int[] right = new int[1];
  if (!balanced_depth(root.left, left)) {
    return false;
  }
  if (!balanced_depth(root.right, right)) {
    return false;
  }
  depth[0] = 1 + Math.max(left[0], right[0]);
  if (Math.abs(left[0] - right[0]) > 1) {
    return false;
  }
  return true;
}

boolean balanced(Node root) {
  int[] depth = new int[1];
  return balanced_depth(root, depth);
}
```

In this solution we use a helper method for the recursive depth calculation. Note that since `Java` does not allow primitives or immutable objects by reference, we wrap the primitive integer within an `int[]` to pass the depth by reference.

3.3.4 Ancestry

The ancestry of a node in a binary tree is the path from the root to the node. A mathematical property of a tree is that there is exactly one simple path between any two nodes in a tree. The calculation of ancestry in a binary search tree is extremely efficient. We need only store the search path used in the find operation.

Listing 3.13: Find Path from Root to Node

```
boolean find_path(Node root,
                  Node target,
                  List<Node> path) {
  if (target == null) {
    return true;
  }
  while (null != root
         && (path.isEmpty()
             || path.get(path.size() - 1)
                != target)) {
    path.add(root);
    if (target.value < root.value) {
      root = root.left;
    } else {
      root = root.right;
    }
  }
  if (path.get(path.size() - 1) == target) {
    return true;
  } else {
    path.clear();
    return false;
  }
}
```

Notice that in this solution, we provide the caller with more information than is necessary. If the node is found in the tree, then we return true. When we return false, the path provided is the ancestry of the node if it were to be inserted in the binary search tree.

Ancestry in a binary tree requires more computation, but could be accomplished with a depth first search.

3.3.5 Lowest common ancestor

The lowest common ancestor of two nodes in a binary tree is the last common node in the paths from the root to each node. This node can be found by using our previous implementation of `find_path`. Having calculated the path from the root to a node, we can compare the two paths until they diverge.

Listing 3.14: Lowest Common Ancestor from Path to Root

```
Node lca_from_path(Node root, Node x, Node y) {
  List<Node> x_path = new ArrayList<Node>();
  List<Node> y_path = new ArrayList<Node>();
  find_path(root, x, x_path);
  find_path(root, y, y_path);
  Node lca = null;
  Iterator<Node> x_path_iterator =
    x_path.iterator();
  Iterator<Node> y_path_iterator =
    y_path.iterator();
  Node current_x, current_y;
  while (x_path_iterator.hasNext()
         && y_path_iterator.hasNext()) {
    current_x = x_path_iterator.next();
    current_y = y_path_iterator.next();
    if (current_x != current_y) {
      break;
    }
    lca = current_x;
  }
  return lca;
}
```

This solution works for binary trees, but in binary search trees there is a solution that does not require pre-generating either path from the root to the nodes. If we were to consider calculating the paths in tandem, a node would be in both paths only if both parameters were left children or right children of the target node. This observation leads to a recursive solution.

Listing 3.15: Lowest Common Ancestor Recursive

```
Node lca_recursive(Node root, Node x, Node y) {
  if (root.value == x.value
      || root.value == y.value) {
    return root;
  }
  if ((x.value < root.value
        && y.value >= root.value)
      || (y.value < root.value
        && x.value >= root.value)) {
    return root;
  }
  if (x.value < root.value) {
    return lca_recursive(root.left, x, y);
  }
  return lca_recursive(root.right, x, y);
}
```

An iterative solution to this problem is easier than iterative solutions to calculating size or paths. Since determining the least common ancestor does not require keeping state, we have no need of an ancillary queue or stack.

Listing 3.16: Lowest Common Ancestor Iterative

```
Node lca_iterative(Node root, Node x, Node y) {
  if (null != x
      && null != y
      && x.value > y.value) {
    Node temp = y;
    y = x;
    x = temp;
  }
  while (null != root
         && root.value != x.value
         && root.value != y.value
         && (y.value < root.value
             || x.value >= root.value)) {
    if (y.value < root.value) {
      root = root.left;
    } else {
      root = root.right;
    }
  }
  return root;
}
```

3.4 Reconstruction

This final discussion of trees deals with the question of how to reconstruct a binary tree from a traversal. This question was a favorite of interviewers at Google for some time. We begin with a discussion of the types of traversals available for a binary tree.

3.4.1 Traversal

As we have seen, many algorithms on binary trees require enumeration of the nodes instead of a search. An enumeration of the nodes in which each data member is visited is called a traversal. We have seen two iterative traversals of a tree above, breadth-first traversal was used to iteratively calculate the size of a tree and depth-first traversal was used to iteratively calculate the depth of a tree.

Traversal of a binary tree is easily accomplished by recursion.

At any node recursively visit the children nodes. It is the order in which nodes are visited which differentiates the three binary tree traversals. These are in-order traversal, post-order traversal, and pre-order traversal.

An in-order traversal guarantees that the data members of a binary search tree will be visited in their sort order. This is accomplished by first recursing left, visiting the current node, and then recursing right.

Listing 3.17: In-Order Traversal

```
void inorder(Node root) {
  if (null == root) {
    return;
  }
  inorder(root.left);
  System.out.println(root.value);
  inorder(root.right);
}
```

A post-order traversal evaluates a current node's data value only after recursively visiting both children.

Listing 3.18: Post-Order Traversal

```
void postorder(Node root) {
  if (null == root) {
    return;
  }
  postorder(root.left);
  postorder(root.right);
  System.out.println(root.value);
}
```

A pre-order traversal is the opposite of a post-order traversal. A pre-order traversal evaluates a current nodes data value prior to recursively visiting either children.

Listing 3.19: Pre-Order Traversal

```
void preorder(Node root) {
  if (null == root) {
    return;
  }
  System.out.println(root.value);
  preorder(root.left);
  preorder(root.right);
}
```

Traversals are useful in serializing a tree to a list of values, and every specific type of traversal produces a deterministic list for a given tree. However suppose we have a list containing a traversal of a general binary tree. Even if that list contains only two values, we can reconstruct multiple trees from an in-order traversal. The reason is that the traversal does not specify which element is the root. In the case where the list contains 3 or more values, pre-order and post-order have ambiguity. Pre-order traversals are ambiguous as to whether or not the second element is a right or left child of the root. Post-order traversals are ambiguous as to whether or not the second to last element is a right or left child of the root. Thus, no single traversal is enough to reconstruct a binary tree. This leads us to the next problem.

3.4.2 Reconstructing a tree from a traversal

We show how to reconstruct a binary tree given any two distinct recursive traversals. The key to solving this problem is recognizing the root from one traversal, and then dividing the traversals into left and right sub-trees using the other. In the following, we provide an algorithm for tree reconstruction from an in-order traversal and a pre-order traversal.

In a pre-order traversal, the first element is always the root of the next sub-tree. The ambiguity is whether the next value is a left or right child of the root. In the in-order traversal, given an index in the traversal, all values to the left are in the left sub-tree and all values to the right are in the right sub-tree. In the solution below, we first extract the root from the pre-order traversal. We then find the index of this value in the in-order traversal. If the value does not appear at the beginning of the in-order traversal there is a left sub-tree. If it does not appear at the end, there is a right sub-tree. In either case we extract from each traversal the subsequences corresponding to a sub-tree, and recurse.

Listing 3.20: Reconstruction of a Binary Tree

```
Node reconstruct_tree(List<Integer> inorder,
                      List<Integer> preorder) {
  Node node = null;
  int inorder_pos;
  int preorder_pos;
  List<Integer> left_preorder;
  List<Integer> right_preorder;
  List<Integer> left_inorder;
  List<Integer> right_inorder;
  if ((preorder.size() != 0)
      && (inorder.size() != 0)) {
    node = new Node(preorder.get(0));
    inorder_pos = inorder.indexOf(preorder.get(0));
    left_inorder = inorder.subList(0, inorder_pos);
    right_inorder = inorder.subList(
      inorder_pos + 1,
      inorder.size());
    preorder_pos = left_inorder.size();
    left_preorder = preorder.subList(
      1,
      preorder_pos + 1);
    right_preorder = preorder.subList(
      preorder_pos + 1,
      preorder.size());
    node.left = reconstruct_tree(left_inorder,
                                 left_preorder);
    node.right = reconstruct_tree(right_inorder,
                                  right_preorder);
  }
  return node;
}
```

Similar algorithms can be rewritten for in-order and post-order, as well as pre-order and post-order.

Chapter 4

Queues and Stacks

The next data structures we visit are queues and stacks.

Queues and stacks are ubiquitous in both programming and technical interviews. Queues are used to maintain priority while processing requests. Stacks are fundamental in program evaluation and parsing. Both are used commonly in graphical search and enumeration algorithms.

In this section we will look at the definitions of queues and stacks. We construct implementations of each from elementary data structures. And finally we look at some interesting interview problems that can be solved with queues and stacks.

4.1 Queue

A queue is an abstract data structure that preserves first-in first-out order of its data. The queue data structure has only two basic operations, enqueue and dequeue. Enqueue pushes data to the back of the queue, and dequeue removes data from the front of the queue. In an efficient implementation, these operations complete in constant time.

A queue is easily implemented from a doubly linked-list. Enqueue appends an item to the tail of a list, and dequeue removes the current head node, replacing it with the next node in the list.

The following is a sample implementation of a queue using a `LinkedList`. The enqueue operation is called `push`, and the dequeue operations is called `pop`, which also returns the item removed from the queue. To access data in the queue, we provide a method called `front` which returns the value of the node at the front of the queue without removing it.

Listing 4.1: Queue Class

```
class Queue {
  private List<Integer> list;

  Queue() {
    list = new LinkedList<Integer>();
  }

  void push(int data) {
    list.add(data);
  }

  Integer front() {
    return (list.size() == 0) ? null
                              : list.get(0);
  }

  Integer pop() {
    return (list.size() == 0) ? null
                              : list.remove(0);
  }
}
```

Note that `Java` provides a `Queue` interface with various class implementations.

4.2 Stack

A stack is an abstract data type that provides last-in first-out access to underlying data. Compared with a queue, it provides a kind of reverse access. As with a queue, a stack exposes two operations. These are push and pop. Push stores data onto the top of a stack, and pop removes data from the top of the stack. These operations run in constant time in an efficient implementation.

A stack is easily implemented from a simple linked-list. The list need not be circular or doubly linked as a stack only accesses the head. A push operation inserts a node at the head, and a pop operation removes the head.

The following is a sample implementation of a stack using the linked-list data structure derived previously. To access the data in the stack, we provide a method called `top` which returns the value of the node at the top of the stack. To remove the data at the top of the stack, we provide a method called `pop` which also returns the value of the removed node.

Listing 4.2: Stack Class

```
class Stack {
  private List<Integer> list;

  Stack() {
    list = new LinkedList<Integer>();
  }

  void push(int data) {
    list.add(0, data);
  }

  Integer top() {
    return (list.size() == 0) ? null : list.get(0);
  }

  Integer pop() {
    return (list.size() == 0) ? null
                              : list.remove(0);
  }
}
```

Note that `Java` provides a `Stack` class with `push`, `pop` and other functions.

4.3 Implement a queue using a stack

A common programming question is to implement a queue using a stack. The goal is to show equivalence the power of the two elementary data types.

The key to solving this problem is to understand that stacks and queues are opposite in terms of their access, and that there is no mechanism by which a single stack alone can implement a queue. The solution is to use two stacks to reverse the data.

In the solution below we have two stacks called in-stack and out-stack. The in-stack allows for enqueue in constant time. Each queue push operation is translated into a stack push operation.

To support first-in first-out, when the dequeue operation is taken we must be able to reach to the bottom of the in-stack. To do this, we need only empty the in-stack to the out-stack. Notice the element last in starts on top of in-stack, and after the transfer it is on the bottom of out-stack. The top of out-stack was the first in, so popping this element provides us with a queue. The private method `transfer` consolidates the logic for the data transfer between the two stacks.

Listing 4.3: Implement Queue from a Stack

```
class QueueFromStack {
  private Stack<Integer> instack;
  private Stack<Integer> outstack;

  QueueFromStack() {
    instack = new Stack<Integer>();
    outstack = new Stack<Integer>();
  }

  void push(int data) {
    instack.push(data);
  }

  Integer front() {
    if (outstack.empty() && instack.empty()) {
      return null;
    }
    transfer();
    return outstack.peek();
  }

  Integer pop() {
    if (outstack.empty() && instack.empty()) {
      return null;
    }
    transfer();
    return outstack.pop();
  }

  private void transfer() {
    if (outstack.empty()) {
      while (!instack.isEmpty()) {
        outstack.push(instack.pop());
      }
    }
  }
}
```

Notice that the out-stack is only updated when it is found to be empty during an access or dequeue operation. A commonly made error is to make out-stack a temporary variable. After creation and popping it once, the contents are transferred back into the in-stack. This is potentially wasteful.

4.4 Implement a stack using a queue

A follow-up is to reverse the question, and ask a candidate to implement a stack using a queue. This question has a number of answers. Similar to above, we provide a solution that uses two queues.

In this solution, we maintain the invariant that the queue that is not empty has its elements in reverse order. In that way, a pop operation need only dequeue from the non-empty queue.

For a single element, this is always the case. Now we suppose a second element is pushed. Instead of pushing it onto the non-empty queue, add it to a secondary and empty queue. This will be the first element removed from the secondary queue. We then transfer the first queue to the secondary queue. This leaves us with a single non-empty queue, whose elements are in last-in first-out order. This logic is the core of the `push` method below.

Listing 4.4: Implement Stack from a Queue

```
class StackFromQueue {
  private Queue<Integer> queue1;
  private Queue<Integer> queue2;

  StackFromQueue() {
    queue1 = new LinkedList<Integer>();
    queue2 = new LinkedList<Integer>();
  }

  void push(int data) {
    Queue<Integer> enqueue =
      queue1.isEmpty() ? queue1 : queue2;
    Queue<Integer> dequeue =
      queue1.isEmpty() ? queue2 : queue1;
    enqueue.add(data);
    while (!dequeue.isEmpty()) {
      enqueue.add(dequeue.poll());
    }
  }

  Integer top() {
    return !queue1.isEmpty()
      ? queue1.peek()
      : queue2.peek();
  }

  Integer pop() {
    return !queue1.isEmpty() ? queue1.poll()
                             : queue2.poll();
  }
}
```

4.5 Level order traversal

A classic interview question is to perform a level order traversal of a binary tree. That is, given a binary tree, visit the nodes from left to right in order of their depth.

The key to solving this question is to use a queue to manage the frontier of exploration. We initialize the queue with the root node. This is the first level. Then each node is visited in turn and its children are enqueued. Every level is contiguous, and levels are visited in turn.

Listing 4.5: Level Order Traversal

```
void level_traversal(Node root) {
  if (null == root) {
    return;
  }
  Queue<Node> queue = new LinkedList<Node>();
  queue.add(root);
  while (!queue.isEmpty()) {
    Node node = queue.poll();
    if (null != node.left) {
      queue.add(node.left);
    }
    if (null != node.right) {
      queue.add(node.right);
    }
    System.out.println(node.value);
  }
}
```

Another name for this enumeration is breadth-first traversal. And we've shown that breadth-first on a binary tree is exactly level order.

A common modification to the question is to separate the levels with a token, such as a newline. In order to accomplish this, we can seed the queue with a level end token such as `null` or a special symbol like `LEVEL_TOKEN`. When we encounter this token again we know that the current level has been fully enumerated. If the token is then enqueued again, it will be placed at the end of the level which was just enqueued. With this trick, we can complete the solution using `LEVEL_TOKEN` as our level separation token.

Listing 4.6: Level Order Traversal with Separation Tokens

```
static final Node LEVEL_TOKEN = new Node(null);

void level_traversal_with_separation_token(
    Node root) {
  if (null == root) {
    return;
  }
  Queue<Node> queue = new LinkedList<Node>();
  queue.add(root);
  queue.add(LEVEL_TOKEN);
  while (!queue.isEmpty()) {
    Node node = queue.poll();
    if (LEVEL_TOKEN == node) {
      if (!queue.isEmpty()) {
        System.out.println("END LEVEL");
        queue.add(LEVEL_TOKEN);
      }
      continue;
    }
    if (null != node.left) {
      queue.add(node.left);
    }
    if (null != node.right) {
      queue.add(node.right);
    }
    System.out.println(node.value);
  }
}
```

4.6 Largest rectangle under a histogram

A histogram is a graphical representation of data in which sequential entries along the x-axis are associated with a height in the y-axis. These values are plotted as rectangles of equal width with height equal to the y-value. In statistics, a histogram gives a graphical representation of a probability distribution.

An advanced interview question is to calculate the area of the largest rectangle under the histogram.

Since the histogram is composed of rectangles, we see that

every maximal rectangle is bounded by the height of some entry in the histogram. The width of every maximal rectangle under the histogram is the number of other rectangles that are contiguous but at least as tall. So we are looking for rectangles bounded by three entries in the histogram: an entry that defines the height, the first contiguous entry of at least that height, and the last contiguous entry of at least that height.

We begin by defining a histogram as a class with x and y coordinates.

Listing 4.7: Definition of `Histogram`

```
class HistogramEntry {
  int x;
  int y;

  HistogramEntry(int x, int y) {
    this.x = x;
    this.y = y;
  }
}
```

A naive solution starts by enumerating all pairs of histogram entries α and β. It calculates the minimum height between α and β by iteratively checking each of those values. The area is then computed and a running max is tracked. However, this solution is cubic!

Using a stack, we can find a solution that solves the problem in a single pass. The stack maintains a collection of all 'open' rectangles. The solution takes it in turn to inspect each entry of the histogram from left to right. When the height of histogram entries is increasing, an open rectangle is added to the stack. It is specified by its x and y coordinates. But the y coordinate must be the earliest rectangle preceding the entry that is at least as tall. We will see that the y coordinate can be determined by closing open rectangles before pushing the new entry onto the stack.

When the height of histogram entry decreases during enumeration, all open entries with height larger than the current value must be closed. The area of an open entry is its height multiplied by width. The width is simply the current x location minus the starting location.

After the last entry has been visited, a final pass must close all open entries.

Listing 4.8: Largest Rectangle Under Histogram

```
int largest_area(List<HistogramEntry> histogram) {
  int max_area = 0;
  int current_pos = 0;
  int last_closed_pos = 0;
  Stack<HistogramEntry> open_entries =
    new Stack<HistogramEntry>();
  for (HistogramEntry entry : histogram) {
    current_pos = entry.x;
    last_closed_pos = entry.x;
    while (!open_entries.isEmpty()
           && open_entries.peek().y >= entry.y) {
      HistogramEntry top = open_entries.pop();
      last_closed_pos = top.x;
      int area =
        top.y * ((current_pos - 1) - (top.x - 1));
      max_area = Math.max(max_area, area);
    }
    open_entries.push(new HistogramEntry(
      last_closed_pos, entry.y));
  }
  current_pos++;
  while (!open_entries.isEmpty()) {
    HistogramEntry top = open_entries.pop();
    int area =
      top.y * ((current_pos - 1) - (top.x - 1));
    max_area = Math.max(max_area, area);
  }
  return max_area;
}
```

In this solution, it is clear that every rectangle is only considered once. This means that every entry in the histogram has been pushed once and popped once, and so we have achieved a linear time algorithm. This is a dramatic improvement over the naive cubic time solution.

Chapter 5

Heaps

In this chapter we examine the heap data structure. The heap, also known as a priority queue, has applications in graph algorithms, caching, and sorting. We begin by discussing multiple variations of the heap. We then examine an implementation the standard operations of the binary heap. And finally, we look at a number of interview problems that can be solved by clever applications of a heap.

5.1 Definition

A heap is an abstract data structure similar to a binary search tree. Like a binary tree, a heap is a collection of nodes that have a data member value and at most two child nodes. The differentiating factor is that nodes in a heap satisfy the heap property. The heap property is held when `p.value` $\geq$ `n.value` for each child node `n` of a parent `p`. A heap that satisfies this property is called a max heap. A min heap satisfies the heap property wherein a parent's data value never exceeds any child's data value. Note that the root of a min heap has the smallest value in the data structure, and the root of a max heap has the largest value in the data structure.

The heap operations are `insert`, `find_max`, `remove_max`, and `increase_key`. The names are self-descriptive of the operations. By maintaining the heap property as an invariant, the `find_max` operation runs in constant time.

Heaps have a number of variants with different worst case running time for other operations. The Brodal heap is a complex collection of algorithms that obtains optimal worst case run time for heap operations. The Brodal heap has constant time implementation `insert`, `find_max`, and `increase_key`. For `remove_max`, we use the Brodal variant to obtain a logarithmic run time.

A second variant is the Fibonacci heap. The Fibonacci heap is so named because it creates and maintains a forest of trees where the numbers of children of the root nodes are bounded below by Fibonacci constants. The relationship between the trees maintains the heap property. The Fibonacci heap achieves only amortized asymptotically optimal bounds on running time for the heap operations. This is a trade-off between complexity of implementation and efficiency.

A simpler variant is the binary heap. In the binary heap, there is a single binary tree structure. The tree structure is always balanced, and grows by insertion in level order. While the binary heap is simple to implement and understand, it does not achieve the asymptotic efficiency of the other variants. Namely, while `find_max` takes constant time and `remove_max` achieves logarithmic time, all other operations in a binary heap have at least logarithmic time lower bounds.

Throughout this section we will take a closer look at the binary heap.

5.2 Operations

In the following section we implement the basic operations for the binary heap: `insert`, `find_max`, `remove_max`, and `increase_key`. Each operates on a binary tree node satisfying the heap property. We begin therefore with the `heapify` operation which can initialize a binary heap from a `List` in-place.

5.2.1 Initialization

Initialization of a binary heap from a `List` involves a logical representation of a binary tree and reordering of the elements so that they satisfy the heap property. We begin by describing the binary tree structure used to represent the heap.

The binary tree structure comes from corresponding the index of entries in the `List` to level order position of nodes in a complete binary tree. Index 0 of the `List` corresponds to the root of the binary tree. For a node at position i in the `List`, the left child is at position $2 * i + 1$, and the right child is at $2 * i + 2$. It will be useful to have a method that computes these indexes.

Listing 5.1: Heap Index of Children

```
int lchild_index(int index) {
  return (index * 2) + 1;
}

int rchild_index(int index) {
  return (index * 2) + 2;
}
```

Notice with this scheme the next available leaf node is the rightmost element passed the end of the heap. The parent of a node at index i is located at $(i - 1)/2$. Integer division achieves rounding down.

Listing 5.2: Heap Index of Parent

```
int parent_index(int index) {
  return (index != 0) ? (index - 1) / 2 : 0;
}
```

Creating the heap starts with the single element of the `List` at index 0. This single element sub-array trivially satisfies the heap property. The operation next iteratively adds elements from the `List` in such a way that the heap property is maintained. Concretely, new elements are first added as leaves. Afterward, parent and child pairs are repeatedly swapped if in violation of the heap property. When the algorithm terminates, the maximum value of the heap is at the first index and the heap property holds.

Listing 5.3: Heap Creation

```
void heapify(List<Integer> array) {
  for (int i = 0; i < array.size(); i++) {
    int parent = parent_index(i);
    while (i != parent
           && array.get(parent) < array.get(i)) {
      int temp = array.get(i);
      array.set(i, array.get(parent));
      array.set(parent, temp);
      i = parent;
      parent = parent_index(i);
    }
  }
}
```

While a binary heap is not an optimally efficient heap structure, as we see the binary heap can be constructed in-place instead of requiring memory allocation for the tree. The time savings realized from not having to allocate ancillary objects often overcome the disadvantage of using an implementation not optimized for worst case behavior.

5.2.2 Insertion

Insertion of a new value into a binary heap begins with adding the value as the next available leaf node in the binary tree. Afterward, the parent-child relationships are updated to satisfy the heap property as was done in creating the heap. Insertion requires the `List` to be dynamically resized, and hence is not an in-place operation.

Listing 5.4: Insert Into a Heap

```
void insert(List<Integer> heap, int value) {
  heap.add(value);
  int index = heap.size() - 1;
  int parent = parent_index(index);
  while (index != 0
         && heap.get(index) > heap.get(parent)) {
    int temp = heap.get(index);
    heap.set(index, heap.get(parent));
    heap.set(parent, temp);
    index = parent;
    parent = parent_index(index);
  }
}
```

5.2.3 Find maximum element

In a binary heap, the `find_max` operation requires only returning the first index of the `List`. Correctness of this action is guaranteed by the heap property.

Listing 5.5: Find Maximum in a Heap

```
int find_max(List<Integer> heap) {
  return heap.get(0);
}
```

5.2.4 Remove maximum element

Removal of the maximum heap value must accomplish two objectives aside from replacing the value at the initial position. First, it must promote the second minimum value to the first position. Doing so causes the tree to pivot, and may have a cascading effect on the structure of the heap. Secondly, the tree structure and parent-child relationships must be maintained.

Both requirements are satisfied by the following sequence. First replace the root value of the heap with the value of the last leaf node, and then resize the array to the smaller size. This maintains the tree structure and removes the maximum element from the array. We are required to then fix up the heap property. In this operation, the heap property is maintained by iteratively swapping parent-child pairs if in violation of the heap property.

Listing 5.6: Remove Maximum from a Heap

```
void remove_max(List<Integer> heap) {
  heap.remove(0);
  int index = 0;
  while (index < heap.size()) {
    int child = lchild_index(index);
    if (child >= heap.size()) {
      break;
    }
    int right = rchild_index(index);
    if (right < heap.size()
        && heap.get(right) > heap.get(child)) {
      child = right;
    }
    if (heap.get(index) >= heap.get(child)) {
      break;
    }
    int temp = heap.get(index);
    heap.set(index, heap.get(child));
    heap.set(child, temp);
    index = child;
  }
}
```

5.2.5 Increase key

When a key is increased in a max heap, the heap property may no longer hold for that node and its parent. Hence, by increasing the value of a key, we may need to decrease its index repeatedly until the array again has the heap property. This is done by our standard practice of iteratively swapping.

Listing 5.7: Increase a Key in a Heap

```
void increase_key(List<Integer> heap, int index) {
  heap.set(index, heap.get(index) + 1);
  int parent = parent_index(index);
  while (0 != index
         && heap.get(index) > heap.get(parent)) {
    int temp = heap.get(index);
    heap.set(index, heap.get(parent));
    heap.set(parent, temp);
    index = parent;
    parent = parent_index(index);
  }
}
```

This operation generalizes to decrease key and key change in the obvious ways.

5.3 Enumeration of powers

Solving programming problems relies as much upon choosing the correct data structure as it does the proper algorithm. Consider the problem of enumerating powers of an initial set of non-negative numbers. Concretely, given a set of integers the question is to list the powers of the integers in increasing order without duplicates. For example, given the set of $2, 3, 4$, the first six powers would be $1 = 2^0, 2 = 2^1, 3 = 3^1, 4 = 4^1 = 4, 8 = 2^3, 9 = 3^2$. We will define the following class to represent the number value and power term pair.

Listing 5.8: ValueTerm Pair

```
class ValueTerm<V, T> {
  private V value;
  private T term;

  ValueTerm(V value, T term) {
    this.value = value;
    this.term = term;
  }
}
```

Enumerating the powers can be solved by using a priority queue pairing a term and its lowest unvisited power.

Listing 5.9: Enumeration of Powers

```
void enumerate_powers(Set<Integer> set,
                              int num_powers,
                              List<Integer> out) {
  PriorityQueue<ValueTerm<Integer,
                              Integer>> heap =
    new PriorityQueue<ValueTerm<Integer,
                                   Integer>>(
      set.size(),
      new Comparator<ValueTerm<Integer,
                                   Integer>>() {
        public int compare(ValueTerm<Integer,
                                      Integer> a,
                           ValueTerm<Integer,
                                      Integer> b) {
          return a.value - b.value;
        }
      });
  for (Integer value : set) {
    heap.add(new ValueTerm<Integer,
                           Integer>(1, value));
  }
  int value = 0;
  while (0 != num_powers && 0 != heap.size()) {
    ValueTerm<Integer, Integer> entry =
      heap.poll();
    if (value != entry.value) {
      value = entry.value;
      out.add(value);
      num_powers--;
    }
    heap.add(new ValueTerm<Integer, Integer>(
      entry.value * entry.term, entry.term));
  }
}
```

Note that by preserving the heap between calls, the solution can be converted to a generator.

5.4 Find top k elements

Finally, let's consider the problem of determining the top k elements of a stream. Online algorithms with stream inputs usually constrain the problem to a single pass, as either the data is volatile or too large to fit into main memory.

Let's begin by reviewing the simple case of finding the maximum element. The maximum element of an array can be found by a linear scan.

Listing 5.10: Find Max Value in an Array

```
int max(int[] array) {
  int max_val = array[0];
  for (int i = 0; i < array.length; i++) {
    max_val = Math.max(array[i], max_val);
  }
  return max_val;
}
```

A little intuition leads us to recall that a single element array is a trivial priority queue. The generalization of this process to finding the top k elements of an n element stream is solved in a single pass with a min heap. To operate within the constraints of memory, we will bound size of the priority queue.

To operate on a bounded size heap, we only insert when the value of an item is larger than the smallest element in the heap. When it is, we remove the smallest element with a `remove_max` operation and then insert the new value.

Listing 5.11: Find Top k Elements of a Stream

```
void find_top_k(InputStream in,
                int k,
                PriorityQueue<Integer> heap)
    throws IOException {
  int val = 0;
  while (heap.size() < k
         && (val = in.read()) != -1) {
    heap.add(val);
  }
  while (in.available() > 0
         && (val = in.read()) != -1) {
    if (val > heap.peek()) {
      heap.poll();
      heap.add(val);
    }
  }
}
```

The run time of this algorithm is an efficient $O(\log k * n)$, as each removal of the minimum element and insertion may take time logarithmic in the size of the heap. This is efficient for the online problem.

Chapter 6

Hash Tables

Hash tables are important data structures whose efficiency and flexibility allow them to be used in almost any kind of search problem.

A large part of being a computer programming is being able to evaluate a problem and design the proper data structure to address it. As the popularity of higher-level languages grows, more and more candidates default to the hash table. Because of their flexibility, hash tables can lead to a correct, but inefficient solution. They can be equally effective in finding duplicates in a linked-list, counting the elements in a stream, and searching a pre-generated list. But hash tables have drawbacks. They cannot be easily enumerated by key or value. It takes work to guarantee a proper hash function has been chosen for a specific data set, as collisions in the search space can degrade lookup performance tremendously. Also there is much memory overhead to using a hash table as a key-value map, and dynamic resizing can occur at any insert.

In this section we cover the material that every candidate should know regarding hash tables. We discuss the three important features of hash table implementation; the hash function, collision resolution, and dynamic resizing. And finally conclude with a number of applications of hash tables that have been asked as interview questions.

6.1 The hash function

A hash function maps a large domain to a smaller range of values. For instance, a simple hash function can map the set of all strings to the integers between 0 and 31. The hash of a data structure is computed by calling a hash function on a specified element of the data structure called a key. The hash value of a variable is the result of evaluating the hash function on that variable's key.

Hash functions require a number of properties to guarantee correctness and efficiency of a hash table.

A hash function must be deterministic in that every data structure with the same key must have the same hash value. Otherwise retrieval from a hash table is impossible.

A hash function should guarantee that the domain is nearly uniformly distributed across the range. That means the probability that two elements, chosen at random, have identical hash values is n^{-1} when the range is of size n. In this way, that hash function minimizes the chance of false positives. A collision is when two distinct elements have equal hash values.

Finally, a hash function must be able to be efficiently computed across the domain. It is common for a hash function to take constant time on elements of the domain.

Hash functions may have other properties, but they find use in only special purposes. For instance a hash function can be tolerant of unimportant features of a key, such as capitalization, to provide normalized hashing. A hash function can be continuous, in that small changes to a key result in small changes to its hash value. This guarantees locality of similar objects within a hash table. Consistent hashing provides a balanced load across a set of ranges, and is used in load balancing client requests.

Let's examine the problem of creating a hash function for lower case English words. Below is a first attempt. Here we hash any lower case English string to the `ASCII` value of its first character.

Listing 6.1: A Simple Hash Function

```
int hash_simple(String str) {
  if (str.isEmpty()) {
    return 0;
  }
  return str.charAt(0) - 'a';
}
```

This function is deterministic and extremely efficient, its range is limited to only 26 values and hence many strings will hash to the same value. Further, the corpus of English words is not uniformly distributed across these 26 values. An examination of the words in the Gutenberg library shows that 17% of the words start with *t*, nearly 12% of words start with the letter *a* but only 0.05% of words start with z.

To overcome these two problems, we add complexity to the calculation of the hash value.

Listing 6.2: Another Hash Function

```
int hash(String str) {
  int hash_value = 0;
  for (int i = 0; i < str.length(); i++) {
    hash_value += str.charAt(i) - 'a';
  }
  return hash_value;
}
```

While this function has a larger range, however it is still small and rather sparse. Also it no longer guarantees constant time operation. The hash value of an extremely long word takes much more time to compute than the hash value of a short word. To overcome these drawbacks, let's consider taking each four character set of characters from the word cast them as an integer. This significantly increases the range. We can sum these sets to distribute the words over the range. And to guarantee constant time operation we bound the number of characters used.

Listing 6.3: Complex Hash Table

```
int hash_complex(String str) {
  int hash_value = 0;
  for (int i = 0, count = 15;
       i < str.length() && count >= 0;
       i++, count--) {
    hash_value += (str.charAt(i) - 'a')
      << (count % 4);
  }
  return hash_value;
}
```

This is better because it maintains a constant time evaluation and we are increasing the range.

It is common that complexity increases as we aim to smooth the distribution or increase the range. With greater complexity comes longer run time, and an unfortunate choice of hash functions can decrease the promise of constant time lookup.

6.2 Definition

A hash table stores elements in an array indexed by their hash value. Each entry in the array is called a bucket. Each element is associated with a key that is used to uniquely identify the bucket that stores the element. The hash function maps the element's key to the bucket in which to store the element. The goal of hash functions is to provide constant time retrieval of stored elements while minimizing insertion time.

In the sequel we will use the `Item` object for elements of the hash table. The key is a string member of an `Item`. Of course in practice, such a definition would be more complex.

Listing 6.4: Definition of `Item` object

```
class Item {
  String key;
  int value;

  Item(String key, int value) {
    this.key = key;
    this.value = value;
  }
}
```

With that defined, a hash table includes a collection of `Item` objects and exposes functions for `hash_function`, `get`, `set`, and `size`. We illustrate this in the following abstract class.

Listing 6.5: Definition of Hashtable

```
abstract class HashTable {
  protected static final int
    DEFAULT_HASH_TABLE_SIZE = ...;

  int hash_function(String str) {
    return ...;
  }

  abstract void insert(Item entry);
  abstract Item find(String key);
  abstract int size();
  abstract void resize(int size);
}
```

A simple hash table implementation can use a `List` to store the collection of `Item` objects.

Listing 6.6: Simple Hashtable

```
class SimpleHashTable extends HashTable {
  private List<Item> items;

  SimpleHashTable() {
    this(DEFAULT_HASH_TABLE_SIZE);
  }

  SimpleHashTable(int size) {
    this.items = new ArrayList<Item>(
      Collections.nCopies(size, (Item)null));
  }

  Item get(int index) {
    return (index < size()) ? items.get(index)
                            : null;
  }

  void set(int index, Item item) {
    items.set(index, item);
  }

  int size() {
    return items.size();
  }

  ...
}
```

Notice that the hash function is defined to take a key type instead of an `Item`. This is because we want to use the same hash function for both insertion and retrieval. Also, we take the liberty of storing object references instead of values in the hash table. While it is true that Item is plain old data and simple to copy, hash tables often contain complex data structures for which it is better to store references instead of copies. We take this approach in this chapter.

6.3 Operations

The two basic operations of a hash table are insertion and retrieval. A third operation often required is dynamic resizing. It is used to increase the capacity and decrease the load of a hash table. By growing the table, it is the goal that the chance of collisions is reduced.

Hash table implementations may also provide access to enumerating the elements of a hash table. This can be done by allowing enumeration of the buckets or by providing direct access to the underlying array. However there is rarely a guarantee that the elements are provided in any sorted order.

Below we provide implementations of `insert`, `find`, and `resize` for our simple hash table.

6.3.1 Insertion

The `insert` operation for a hash table requires calculating hash values and addressing collisions if they occur. Collision resolution is discussed in another section below. This listing provides an incomplete hash table implementation that does not guarantee retrieval of stored elements. Instead we evict older entries when collisions are detected. Such a scheme is useful in cache implementations, but not as useful for using hash tables for histograms.

Note that in order to convert the hash value to a valid index, we mod out the hash value by the size of the `List`.

Listing 6.7: Insert into a Hashtable

```
void insert(Item entry) {
  int index = hash_function(entry.key) % size();
  set(index, entry);
}
```

6.3.2 Retrieval

Implementing the `find` operation in a hash table depends on the hash value of a key and the insertion scheme. As multiple keys can hash to the same value, it is important that retrieval determine if an entry agrees with the key used in retrieval. For that reason there is an equality check after retrieval by index.

Listing 6.8: Find in a Hashtable

```
Item find(String key) {
  int index = hash_function(key) % size();
  Item item = get(index);
  return item != null && item.key.equals(key)
    ? item
    : null;
}
```

6.3.3 Dynamic resizing

Commonly, a hash table exposes a third method for dynamic resizing. Dynamic resizing refers to increasing the size of the underlying data structure while maintaining the key to hash value mapping of the table. There are two steps. The first is allocation of a new buffer to store the elements. And the second is a rehashing of the elements in the original table to the second.

Listing 6.9: Dynamic Resizing of a Hashtable

```
void resize(int size) {
  List<Item> new_table = new ArrayList<Item>(
    Collections.nCopies(size, (Item)null));
  for (Item entry : this.items) {
    if (null != entry) {
      new_table.set(
        hash_function(entry.key) % size,
        entry);
    }
  }
  this.items = new_table;
}
```

During dynamic resizing, a rehash is necessary. Because of this it is sometimes beneficial to update the hash function at the same time. Such an update may be as simple as changing an offset for the hash value calculation.

While this implementation provides a possibly lossy implementation of a hash table, any of the collision resolution schemes below guarantee retrieval of all elements inserted into the hash table.

6.4 Collision resolution

Collision resolution refers to a scheme for dealing with collisions in hash table insertion. In the simple example above, the hash table was not correct in the sense that subsequent inserts in the event of a hash collision could evict objects stored in the hash table. Below we will discuss and implement three popular and efficient schemes for collision resolution.

6.4.1 Separate chaining

Separate chaining is the most commonly taught method of collision resolution. With separate chaining, the buckets of the hash table contain linked-lists that hold the keys. This provides unlimited capacity for the hash table. However, it comes at the cost of increased lookup time as the hash table becomes filled to capacity. In the worst case, lookup time can become linear.

To implement separate chaining we modify the definition of a hash table so that the underlying data structure contains lists of `Item` references.

Listing 6.10: Definition of Hashtable with Separate Chaining

```
class SeparateChainingHashTable
    extends HashTable {
  private List<List<Item>> items;

  SeparateChainingHashTable() {
    this(DEFAULT_HASH_TABLE_SIZE);
  }

  SeparateChainingHashTable(int size) {
    this.items = new ArrayList<List<Item>>(
      Collections.nCopies(size,
                          new LinkedList<Item>()));
  }

  List<Item> get(int index) {
    return (index < items.size())
      ? items.get(index)
      : null;
  }

  void set(int index, Item item) {
    items.get(index).add(item);
  }

  ...
}
```

When an element is inserted into a hash table with separate chaining, it is simply pushed onto the list stored at the bucket. This provides constant time insertion. It also guarantees that an item can be retrieved once it has been inserted as there is no eviction.

Listing 6.11: Insert with Separate Chaining

```
void insert(Item entry) {
  int index = hash_function(entry.key) % size();
  set(index, entry);
}
```

Retrieval from separate chaining requires enumerating the lists to complete the search for an entry. As above, we must ensure the element's key matches the parameter. That this requirement is clear, as with separate chaining it is common for the table to have multiple entries with the same hash value.

Listing 6.12: Find with Separate Chaining

```
Item find(String key) {
  int index = hash_function(key) % size();
  List<Item> itemsList = get(index);
  for (Item i : itemsList) {
    if (i.key.equals(key)) {
      return i;
    }
  }
  return null;
}
```

Dynamic resizing with separate chaining takes only a little more effort, as each list in each bucket must be enumerated. Aside from this caveat, implementation of dynamic resizing is straightforward.

6.4.2 Open addressing

Open addressing is a scheme by which collisions are resolved by inserting an element at the next available bucket in the hash table given some iteration scheme. Commonly, open addressing involves simply iterating through the table. This is called open addressing with linear probing. However, open addressing can be implemented by other probing schemes such as successively doubling the index value. If no available bucket is found, the table is dynamically resized and the insert resumes. Note that after resizing, we are guaranteed to find an available bucket. Dynamically resizing and a possible linear time enumeration are the cost the hash table pays for guaranteeing retrieval.

We implement a hash table supporting open addressing with linear probing. Insertion is only a matter of finding an open bucket.

Listing 6.13: Insert with Open Addressing

```
void insert(Item entry) {
  while (true) {
    int index = hash_function(entry.key) % size();
    for (int offset = 0;
         offset < size();
         offset++) {
      int bucket_index = (index + offset) % size();
      if (null == get(bucket_index)) {
        set(bucket_index, entry);
        return;
      }
    }
    resize(size() * 2 + 1);
  }
}
```

To ensure that a false negative is not returned on lookup, an open addressing scheme must iterate through all successive buckets to ensure that an entry is not present at successive location. Caution must be exercised to not loop continuously.

Listing 6.14: Find with Open Addressing

```
Item find(String key) {
  int index = hash_function(key) % size();
  for (int offset = 0;
       offset < size();
       offset++) {
    int bucket_index = (index + offset) % size();
    Item item = get(bucket_index);
    if (null == item) {
      return null;
    }
    if (key.equals(item.key)) {
      return item;
    }
  }
  return null;
}
```

6.4.3 Cuckoo hashing

Cuckoo hashing is a modern approach to collision resolution that provides expected constant time lookup and insertion when the load of the table is low. Instead of linear probing, cuckoo hashing uses a combination of two hash functions and two tables to find the next available bucket for a value. The hash functions and tables are labeled primary and secondary, corresponding to the order they are probed.

To realize expected constant time operations, cuckoo hashing requires a more complex definition for the hash table.

Listing 6.15: Definition of Hashtable with Cuckoo Hashing

```
class CuckooHashTable extends HashTable {
  interface HashFunction {
    int hash_function(String key);
  }

  private List<List<Item>> items;
  private List<HashFunction> hash_functions;

  CuckooHashTable() {
    this(DEFAULT_HASH_TABLE_SIZE);
  }

  CuckooHashTable(int size) {
    this.items = new ArrayList<List<Item>>(2);
    this.items.add(new ArrayList<Item>(
      Collections.nCopies(size, (Item)null)));
    this.items.add(new ArrayList<Item>(
      Collections.nCopies(size, (Item)null)));
  }

  int size() {
    return items.get(0).size();
  }

  ...
}
```

Insertions begin by checking the first table. If the hash value bucket is occupied, its contents are replaced with the new entry and the old entry is promoted to the second table. This process repeats until all entries are added or else an infinite loop is detected. In the latter case, the table is resized and the process continues. In the code below, we use `table_index` to track if we are operating on the primary or secondary table. The set is used to detect if a loop is encountered. Also we use references to make the code easier to read.

Listing 6.16: Insert with Cuckoo Hashing

```
void insert(Item entry) {
  List<Set<Integer>> visited =
    new ArrayList<Set<Integer>>(
      Collections.nCopies(2,
                            new HashSet<Integer>()));
  int table_index = 0;
  int index = 0;
  do {
    List<Item> table = items.get(table_index);
    HashFunction hashfn = hash_functions.get(
      table_index);
    index = hashfn.hash_function(entry.key)
      % table.size();
    Item previous_entry = table.get(index);
    table.set(index, entry);
    if (null == previous_entry) {
      return;
    }
    entry = previous_entry;
    visited.get(table_index).add(index);
    table_index = (0 == table_index) ? 1 : 0;
  } while (
    !visited.get(table_index).contains(index));
  resize(items.get(0).size() * 2 + 1);
  insert(entry);
}
```

The resize is necessary if an infinite loop is detected. With a poor choice of hash function, it is possible for the insert-resize process to also loop. To insure against this, it is advisable to update the hash function during resize. Other than that, the resize member is straightforward.

Lookup in a hash table with cuckoo hashing must determine if the key is in the first or second table. The latter check is only needed when the hash table bucket in the first table is occupied by an element not equal to the value seen.

Listing 6.17: Find with Cuckoo Hashing

```
Item find(String key) {
  for (int table_index = 0;
       table_index < 2;
       table_index++) {
    List<Item> table = items.get(table_index);
    HashFunction hashfn = hash_functions.get(
      table_index);
    int index = hashfn.hash_function(key)
      % table.size();
    Item item = table.get(index);
    if (null == item) {
      return null;
    }
    if (key.equals(item.key)) {
      return item;
    }
  }
  return null;
}
```

This concludes our overview of the fundamentals of hash tables. Java provides a hash table implementation in its Hashtable class, which we will use when appropriate in the sequel.

6.5 Find the most common elements in a stream

Consider the problem of finding the most common element in large list with many distinct elements.

To solve this problem, we want to build a histogram of the count of each distinct element. To construct this histogram we will require a container to store an entry that is a tuple of the element and a counter. The element is the key of this entry, and the counter is the entry's value.

When elements are first encountered, we add an entry with count 1. Otherwise we increment the counter associated with that element. So clearly, for each element in the list we need to support both insertion and lookup. In a binary tree, each lookup can require order $\log n$ comparisons, and each insert can require order $\log n$ comparisons. An efficient hash table we can reduce each lookup and insertion to expected constant time and solve the problem with a linear scan.

After scanning the input, the hash table has a count of the frequency of each element in the list. We can keep track of the current most common element during iteration. If the k most common elements are desired, we can use a bounded size min heap as in the previous section.

The following listing provides an implementation of finding the most common element in a list of strings using a hash table.

Listing 6.18: Find the Most Common Element

```
String find_most_common_element(
    Scanner in,
    Map<String, Integer> hash_table) {
  String str;
  while (in.hasNext()) {
    str = in.next();
    int previous_count =
      (hash_table.get(str) == null)
        ? 0
        : hash_table.get(str);
    hash_table.put(str, previous_count + 1);
  }
  String max_str = "";
  int max_count = 0;
  for (Map.Entry<String, Integer> entry :
      hash_table.entrySet()) {
    if (entry.getValue() > max_count) {
      max_str = entry.getKey();
      max_count = entry.getValue();
    }
  }
  return max_str;
}
```

6.6 Implement a most recently used cache

A cache is a data structure used to reduce retrieval time of data from a remote store. A subset of elements is stored locally, and retrieval first looks locally before looking remotely. Caches are bounded and store only a subset of the data available from the remote store. For this reason they must implement an eviction policy. A most recently used cache is one that evicts the least recently used element. In this subsection, we solve the problem of implementing a MRU cache.

The MRU cache must efficiently support both retrieval and priority updating. To implement this data type we use a combination of two containers we have already visited. We use the built-in `HashMap` implementation for lookup, and a doubly linked-list to maintain priority.

To facilitate retrieval in the linked-list, the hash table used for retrieval stores references to the nodes of the linked-list. The linked-list stores the priority of each entry in the cache by the order of the nodes. The head of the linked-list always contains the most recently accessed item, and the tail will be the least recently accessed item. In order to maintain correctness, the cache must be updated whenever an element is used.

The structures used in our cache are present in the definition below.

Listing 6.19: Most Recently Used Cache

```
class MruCache {
  private LinkedList<Item> list;
  private Map<String, Item> table;
  private int bound;

  MruCache(int bound) {
    list = new LinkedList<Item>();
    table = new HashMap<String, Item>();
    this.bound = bound;
  }

  ...
}
```

The MRU cache also implements two methods, `find` and `store`. The `find` method uses the hash table for quick retrieval of items from the cache. When `find` retrieves an item, that item is accessed and the priority must be updated. To update the priority without allocating new memory, we move the location of the item's node within the linked-list to the head.

Listing 6.20: Retrieval in Most Recently Used Cache

```
Item find(String key) {
  Item item = table.get(key);
  if (null != item) {
    list.remove(item);
    list.offerFirst(item);
    return item;
  }
  return null;
}
```

When local retrieval fails, a method must call the remote store. The item retrieved is then saved to the cache by the `store` function. It is within `store` that the eviction policy is implemented. The item stored is prepended to the front of the list, and the hash table is updated with the item's key value. If the cache is above capacity after the item is added, the least recently used item is removed. This item is found at the tail of the list. When removed from the priority queue, the item must also be removed from the hash table.

Listing 6.21: Access Recording in Most Recently Used Cache

```
void store(Item item) {
  list.push(item);
  table.put(item.key, item);
  if (list.size() > bound) {
    table.remove(list.getLast().key);
    list.removeLast();
  }
}
```

Let's consider the running time of this implementation. The operations of the `find` method are a hash table lookup and moving a node to the head of the linked-list. These are constant time operations. Further, the operations of the `store` method are insertion into the hash table, insertion into a linked-list, and a possible removal from the linked-list. These operations also take constant time. From this we see we have an efficient implementation of the MRU cache.

Chapter 7

Binary Search

Searching and sorting are the fundamental operations of computer programming, and in the next few chapters we examine each in some detail. There are three search techniques that every programmer should memorize. These are binary search, breadth first search, and depth first search. Binary search can be used for search in any sorted, random access data structure. Breadth first search and depth first search are graph search algorithms useful for finding minimum distance between nodes and detecting cycles. Before sorting, we will look at basic implementations and programming problems related to each of these search algorithms.

We begin with binary search.

7.1 Binary search

Binary search is fundamental, and it should be known by rote as it is often asked as a gating or screening question. It is one of the first algorithms we learn, and influences many data structures we use in programming. It is also one for the first applications of branch and bound, in that the update rule divides the search space in half.

The following is an implementation of binary search for searching an integer array. The result of the search is the location of the element with the specified key.

Listing 7.1: Binary Search

```
int find(int[] array, int key) {
  int lower = 0;
  int upper = array.length - 1;
  while (lower < upper) {
    int mid = lower + (upper - lower) / 2;
    if (key == array[mid]) {
      return mid;
    } else if (key < array[mid]) {
      upper = mid - 1;
    } else {
      lower = mid + 1;
    }
  }
  return lower;
}
```

A few details of this implementation require further discussion. First, the function above returns either the position of the entry or the point at which the algorithm was searching when it determined the key is not present. We will see this definition is useful in the sequel.

Second, if we did not find an entry, we know that $key \neq array[mid]$, and so we do not need to consider *mid*. So we can set *lower* and *upper* one past mid in the appropriate direction. Concretely, if the value we are looking for is less than *mid*, we can set *upper* to be $mid - 1$, as that is the lowest index that we have not evaluated.

Last, the update rule used to find the midpoint should always be used in programming interviews. It is the only means to write the expression to calculate the midpoint of a without the danger of an operation overflow. The more common way to write that line is $mid = (upper + lower)/2$. However, it is possible for $upper + lower$ to overflow.

Binary search provides order $\log n$ lookup, and is optimal for comparison search. However while the screening interview may ask for a quick implementation, its specific application to interview problems is sometimes subtle.

7.2 Find the first occurrence in a sorted array

An interview question that can be solved with slight modification to binary search is the problem of finding the leftmost occurrence of a target value n in a sorted array. Modifying both the update rules and the exit criteria of the previous implementation of binary search can solve this question.

While previous implementation of the binary search algorithm provides an incomplete answer, it does provide information on the location of the target. We should immediately see that once we find any index that matches the target value, we could scan linearly until we find the leftmost element with the target value. While this provides a correct solution, the run time of the algorithm is linear.

Note that when an index with the target value is found, we can update *upper* to be that index that we discovered. Doing so would always keep the target solution in range of our search. So we change the line $upper = mid - 1$ to $upper = mid$. The update rule for *lower* need not change. However, we see that if the lower bound is ever equal to the target after an update it must be pointing to the leftmost entry. Our final solution then is a modified binary search.

Listing 7.2: Binary Search to Find Leftmost Target

```
int find_leftmost(int[] array, int key) {
  int lower = 0;
  int upper = array.length - 1;
  while (lower < upper && array[lower] != key) {
    int mid = lower + (upper - lower) / 2;
    if (key <= array[mid]) {
      upper = mid;
    } else {
      lower = mid + 1;
    }
  }
  return lower;
}
```

A similar modification of the update rules can be made to locate the rightmost index with the target value.

7.3 Search in a rotated array

A more complicated question asks the candidate to search for a target value in a sorted array that has been rotated. A rotated array is a sorted array of length n in which every index i has been mapped to index $i + j \pmod{n}$ for some integer value j. Concretely, the array 12345 rotated by 2 is the array 45123.

For simplicity, we assume that there do not exist duplicate values in each given array.

There are two common solutions to this interview question; one requires a complex modification to the update rule. The other requires a two-step search algorithm.

Let's again see what modifications to binary search are required. Given the example above, we immediate see that the problem with our candidate solution is only the update rules. Since we cannot guarantee that array is increasing from *lower* to *mid* and from *mid* to *upper*, we are not updating properly. What is needed is to consider the location of the pivot. By enumerating cases, we can see that the pivot is either in between *lower* and *mid*, *mid* and *upper* or no longer being considered in the sub array that is being searched. Since the array does not contain duplicates, we can determine whether or not the pivot is in the range *lower* to *mid* by testing if $lower < mid$ and if the key is bounded by *lower* and *mid*. This leads to our first solution.

Listing 7.3: Binary Search in Rotated Array

```
int find_rotated(int[] array, int key) {
  int lower = 0;
  int upper = array.length - 1;
  while (lower < upper) {
    int mid = lower + (upper - lower) / 2;
    if (key == array[mid]) {
      upper = mid;
    } else if (array[lower] <= array[mid]) {
      if (array[lower] <= key
          && key < array[mid]) {
        upper = mid;
      } else {
        lower = mid + 1;
      }
    } else if (array[mid] <= array[upper]) {
      if (array[mid] < key
          && key <= array[upper]) {
        lower = mid + 1;
      } else {
        upper = mid;
      }
    }
  }
  return lower;
}
```

Let's consider a second solution by addressing the problem of an unknown pivot another way. If we knew the location of the pivot j, then instead of special casing the ranges of *lower* to *mid* and *mid* to *upper*, we can instead modify the binary search update rule to use modulo arithmetic. Concretely, if n is the length of the array, we could set $lower = j$, $upper = j + n - 1 \pmod{n} = j - 1 \pmod{n}$, and $mid = lower + (upper - lower)/2 \pmod{n}$. Our previous binary search is then correct. This is implemented below.

Listing 7.4: Binary Search with Pivot Offset

```
int find_with_pivot_offset(int[] array,
                           int pivot,
                           int key) {
  int lower = 0;
  int upper = array.length - 1;
  while (lower < upper) {
    int mid = lower + (upper - lower) / 2;
    int mid_val = (mid + pivot) % array.length;
    if (key <= array[mid_val]) {
      upper = mid;
    } else {
      lower = mid + 1;
    }
  }
  return (lower + pivot) % array.length;
}
```

How can we find j? In linear time we can search for the index of the minimum value. However, an optimal method can be built upon binary search using update rules similar to the first solution of this problem. That is we update the lower and upper bounds of a binary search to insure that the pivot is always between them. When this can no longer be satisfied, then the lower bound must be the pivot value.

Listing 7.5: Binary Search for the Pivot in Rotated Array

```
int find_pivot(int[] array) {
  int lower = 0;
  int upper = array.length - 1;
  while (lower < upper) {
    int mid = lower + (upper - lower) / 2;
    if (array[lower] <= array[mid]) {
      if (array[mid] < array[upper]) {
        break;
      }
      lower = mid + 1;
    } else {
      upper = mid;
    }
  }
  return lower;
}
```

7.4 Find a fixed-point

An interesting mathematical programming problem asks the candidate to find the fixed-point in a function.

Concretely, suppose that a monotonically increasing integral function is defined on the integers $[0, 100]$ taking values in $[0, 100]$. It is represented by an array A, where $f(x) = A[x]$. Since the function is bounded and increasing, there must be a value y such that $f(y) = y$. Such a y is called a fixed-point.

We can find the fixed-point with binary search with a process similar to what was used to find the pivot in a rotated array. The idea is to always update the bounds so that the fixed-point is in the range being searched. To do this, we update so that $lower \leq A[lower]$ and $upper \geq A[upper]$. Below is an implementation of this solution.

Listing 7.6: Find a Fixed-Point

```
int fixed_point(int[] array) {
  int lower = 0;
  int upper = array.length - 1;
  while (lower < upper) {
    int mid = lower + (upper - lower) / 2;
    if (array[mid] <= mid) {
      upper = mid;
    } else {
      lower = mid + 1;
    }
  }
  return lower;
}
```

7.5 Find duplicate values

Suppose we are asked to find one value in a sequence of integers that appears twice. We can solve this problem with binary search.

The idea is to update the bounds so that we consider the half that is larger than the number of integers it could hold if there were no duplicates. The reason this works is similar to above. For if there is a duplicate value in the array, and the array has all the elements in the sequence, then the length of the array must be larger than the difference of its last and first elements.

Listing 7.7: Find Duplicates in a Sequence

```
int find_duplicates(int[] array) {
  int lower = 0;
  int upper = array.length - 1;
  while (lower < upper) {
    int mid = lower + (upper - lower) / 2;
    int mid_val = array[lower]
      + (array[upper] - array[lower]) / 2;
    if (mid_val < array[mid]) {
      upper = mid;
    } else {
      lower = mid + 1;
    }
  }
  return lower;
}
```

Note the similarity with finding the fixed-point of a function. The expected middle value is what would be present if there were no duplicates. By calculating it above and comparing against the actual mid, we are converting the bounds so this and the fixed-point problem have the same problem.

7.6 Binary search in a Young Tableau

Finally, let's consider an example that uses the technique of binary search in a more complex implementation. Suppose we are given an $n \times m$ matrix M of integers. The integers are sorted from smallest to largest in columns and in rows. That is $M_{ij} \leq M_{il}$ whenever $j \leq l$, and $M_{ij} \leq M_{kj}$ whenever $i \leq k$. Such a matrix is called a Young tableau. The question is to find the coordinates of an element of the matrix with a specified value.

A coordinate is defined by the following class.

Listing 7.8: Definition of a Coordinate

```
class Coordinate {
  int x;
  int y;

  Coordinate(int x, int y) {
    this.x = x;
    this.y = y;
  }
}
```

And matrix data type we use is defined below.

Listing 7.9: Definition of a Matrix

```
class Matrix {
  int[][] matrix;

  Matrix(int rows, int cols) {
    this.matrix = new int[rows][cols];
  }

  int getRows() {
    return matrix.length;
  }

  int getCols() {
    return getRows() == 0 ? 0 : matrix[0].length;
  }
}
```

We want to choose bounds such that after a comparison the search space can be significantly reduced. If we try to flatten the matrix and search, preprocessing would require visiting all n^2 elements. But we should be able to do better with a kind of binary search.

To apply binary search, we would need to find an update rule that reduces the search space significantly. Suppose we have a midpoint of the matrix at position i, j. If $M[i.j]$ is less than our key value, we could increase the value of the matrix entry. So it is appropriate to increment either the row or column. If $M[i, j]$ is greater than our key value we need to decrement either the row or column. To avoid branching we want to choose a starting position where we have exactly one choice of updates after comparing an entry to the key value. There are two natural locations that provide this property: the bottom left corner and the top right corner. Below we start in the bottom left corner of the matrix and perform a diagonal search upward.

Listing 7.10: Diagonal Search of a Matrix

```
Coordinate matrix_find(Matrix m, int key) {
  int rows = m.getRows();
  int cols = m.getCols();
  Coordinate coord = new Coordinate(rows - 1, 0);
  while (coord.x < rows
         && coord.y < cols
         && m.matrix[coord.x][coord.y] != key) {
    if (m.matrix[coord.x][coord.y] > key) {
      coord.x--;
    } else {
      coord.y++;
    }
  }
  return coord;
}
```

The algorithm above is linear. To see this, note that in the worst case it may traverse to the opposite corner of the matrix. But as we've seen, binary search attains logarithmic run time by reducing the search space by a constant amount. And with some insight that bound can be achieved for search on the Young tableau.

First we will need to find a variant of binary search that returns the location of the first value within a sub-array that is greater than or equal to the search key. This is similar to the `find_leftmost` function derived earlier with the exception that the sub-array boundaries are passed in as parameters.

Listing 7.11: Find Lower Bound

```
int lower_bound(int[] array,
                int lower,
                int upper,
                int key) {
  while (lower < upper) {
    int mid = lower + (upper - lower) / 2;
    if (key <= array[mid]) {
      upper = mid;
    } else {
      lower = mid + 1;
    }
  }
  return lower;
}
```

Now let's consider the extreme matrix entries. $M[1,1]$ is the smallest entry in the matrix, and $M[n,m]$ is the largest. Generalizing, given a sub-matrix defined by entries $M[p,q]$ and $M[s,t]$, where $p \leq s$, and $q \leq t$, we know that $M[p,q]$ is the smallest entry in the sub-matrix and $M[s,t]$ is the largest.

With this insight, we can write a matrix binary search that reduces the search space by a constant fraction each step. This will produce an optimal solution. The idea is to start with a sub matrix bounded by $M[p,q]$ on the top left and $M[s,t]$ on the bottom right. We calculate a middle row $i = (p+s)/2$, and search this row to find the column which best separates the matrix into four sub-matrices. The column j that achieves this is the first entry $M[i,j]$ in row i that is greater than or equal to the key value. Now consider the separation of the matrix into the four sub matrices bounded by row i and column j. The key cannot appear in the top left sub-matrix because it is larger than $M[i-1,j-1]$. Further the key can not appear in the bottom right sub-matrix because it is smaller than $M[i,j]$. Hence we need only look at the remaining two sub-matrices: the upper right and lower left. We have narrowed the search down to half the original domain.

Listing 7.12: Binary Search in Young Tableau

```
boolean recursive_find(Matrix m,
                       int key,
                       Coordinate lower,
                       Coordinate upper,
                       Coordinate out) {
  if (lower.x > upper.x
      || lower.y > upper.y
      || m.getRows() <= Math.max(lower.x, upper.x)
      || m.getCols() <= Math.max(lower.y,
                                 upper.y)) {
    return false;
  }
  int mid_row = lower.x + (upper.x - lower.x) / 2;
  int mid_col = lower_bound(m.matrix[mid_row],
                            lower.y,
                            upper.y,
                            key);
  if (mid_row < m.getRows()
      && mid_col < m.getCols()
      && m.matrix[mid_row][mid_col] == key) {
    out.x = mid_row;
    out.y = mid_col;
    return true;
  }
  return recursive_find(
    m,
    key,
    new Coordinate(mid_row + 1, lower.y),
    new Coordinate(upper.x, mid_col - 1),
    out)
  || recursive_find(
    m,
    key,
    new Coordinate(lower.x, mid_col),
    new Coordinate(mid_row - 1, upper.y),
    out);
}

Coordinate matrix_find_binary_search(Matrix m,
                                     int key) {
  Coordinate lower = new Coordinate(0, 0);
  Coordinate upper = new Coordinate(
    m.getRows() - 1,
    m.getCols() - 1);
  Coordinate out = new Coordinate(0, 0);
  recursive_find(m, key, lower, upper, out);
  return out;
}
```

This poly-logarithmic algorithm above is quite difficult, and may take a couple readings. The best takeaway is that there is oftentimes a best separation of the search space, and that is worth finding.

Chapter 8

Graphical Search

We have already considered search over a binary search tree, now we consider search over general graphs. The most common graphical search algorithms are breadth first search and depth first search. In the following sections, we will look at basic implementation of each of these search algorithms. Afterward we will solve programming problems with these search techniques.

8.1 Definition of a graph

Before we begin, we formally define a graph. A graph is a collection of vertices with edge relations. Two vertices are adjacent if they share an edge between them. Adjacent vertices are called neighbors. In an undirected graph, edges are symmetric relations. That is if a and b are vertices and (a, b) is an edge, then (b, a) is also an edge. A graph is directed if edges are not symmetric. That is if (a, b) is an edge, (b, a) is not necessarily an edge.

We represent graphs with nodes and adjacency lists. Each vertex in a graph will be represented by the following `Node` class.

Listing 8.1: Graph Node

```
class Node {
  int value;
  List<Node> neighbors;

  Node(int value, List<Node> neighbors) {
    this.value = value;
    this.neighbors = neighbors;
  }
}
```

Each node has a value stored. The edges originating at a node are stored in the `List` member `neighbors`. As such, `neighbors` contains the list of all vertices adjacent to the `Node`.

A graph is *connected* if for any pair of vertices a and z in the graph, there is a list of vertices starting with a and ending with z in which every adjacent pair in the list are neighbors. Such a list is called a *path*. A simple path is one that does not intersect itself. A *cycle* in a graph is a list of nodes starting and ending with the same node in which every adjacent pair in the list are neighbors. Trees are connected graphs that do not contain cycles. This allows tree traversal algorithms to not need to worry about infinite loops. However in graph traversals special care must be taken to ensure we do not double back and be caught in an infinite loop.

8.2 Breadth first search

With breadth first search, abbreviated *bfs*, we study our first graph search algorithm. *bfs* starts from an origin node and visits all reachable nodes in a graph in order of their distance from the origin. The number of edges from the origin measures distance. *bfs* is characterized by the use of a queue to maintain the order in which nodes are visited. The queue contains the known frontier of the search, which are all nodes that are known to exist but have not yet been visited.

As mentioned above, graphs can have cycles between the nodes. To avoid doubling back while traversing the graph, *bfs* must keep track of all visited nodes and not add nodes multiple times to the queue. To do this, we use a `Set` to track our history.

As with tree traversal, *bfs* is usually required to do more than simply pop every node from the queue. Often *bfs* is implemented to take a general `visit` function that is called each time a node is examined. We achieve this by implementing the following `Visitor` interface.

Listing 8.2: Visitor Interface

```
interface Visitor {
  public void visit(Node node);
}
```

Using the `Node` class defined previously, we can list an implementation of *bfs* with a parameter called visit.

Listing 8.3: Breadth First Search

```
void bfs(Node origin, Visitor visit) {
  Set<Node> queued = new HashSet<Node>();
  Queue<Node> queue = new LinkedList<Node>();
  queue.add(origin);
  while (!queue.isEmpty()) {
    Node current = queue.poll();
    visit.visit(current);
    for (Node neighbor : current.neighbors) {
      if (!queued.contains(neighbor)) {
        queued.add(current);
        queue.add(neighbor);
      }
    }
  }
}
```

As we will see, it is the visit function that makes `bfs` powerful.

8.2.1 Find the distance between nodes in a graph

Since *bfs* visits each node in order of its distance from the origin, it can be used to solve the problem of finding the minimal distance from an origin to all other nodes in a graph. In doing so we implement a special case of Dijkstra's algorithm for the case where all edges are of equal weight.

The idea is to update the known distance of a node when we first add it to the queue. Doing so will require keeping track of the state of node exploration. The `get_distance` method sets distance of unvisited nodes to infinity. When a node is first encountered, all the children are given distance equal to the distance of the parent plus one. Since *bfs* visits each node in order of its distance, a parent's distance will always be set before a child is encountered. Translating this into code, we have the following listing.

Listing 8.4: Shortest Path Distances

```
class DistanceVisitor implements Visitor {
  private Map<Node, Integer> distances;

  DistanceVisitor(Map<Node, Integer> distances) {
    this.distances = distances;
  }

  public void visit(Node node) {
    if (distances.isEmpty()) {
      distances.put(node, 0);
    }
    for (Node neighbor : node.neighbors) {
      int vertexDistance = distance(distances,
                                    node);
      int neighborDistance =
        distance(distances, neighbor);
      distances.put(neighbor,
                    Math.min(neighborDistance,
                             1 + vertexDistance));
    }
  }

  private int distance(
      Map<Node, Integer> distances,
      Node vertex) {
    Integer distance = distances.get(vertex);
    if (null == distance) {
      return Integer.MAX_VALUE;
    }
    return distance;
  }
}

void find_distances(
    Node origin,
    Map<Node, Integer> distances) {
  Visitor visit = new DistanceVisitor(distances);
  bfs(origin, visit);
}
```

At completion of the algorithm, the parameter `distances` maps nodes to their shortest path distances to the origin.

Tracking and modifying *bfs* to provide state information when visiting a node is a powerful technique that has many other uses.

8.2.2 Ancestry from genealogical data

This interview question asks a candidate to determine if two people are related. We can treat each person as a node. Every node has at most two parents. The question is framed as having incomplete genealogical data, that is, the full ancestry of each individual may not be known. This gives rise to graphs that may not be connected.

To solve this problem, we first represent the domain as a directed graph. Each person is a node, with the key being an identifier for a person. Every node is adjacent to at most two other nodes representing the parents. Edges are orientated from a child to parent. We use a `Map` from child id to parent ids to represent the graph.

To determine whether or not two individuals are related, we first use *bfs* to calculate the full ancestry of each individual. Since we are dealing with a graph represented in a `Map`, *bfs* will need to be modified to understand this representation. The visit function simply adds parents to an instance. In the listing below, we inline the visit function instead of passing it as a parameter.

Listing 8.5: Ancestry from Genealogical Data

```
void find_ancestry(
    Map<Integer, List<Integer>> data,
    int id,
    Set<Integer> ancestry) {
  Queue<Integer> queue = new LinkedList<Integer>();
  queue.add(id);
  ancestry.add(id);
  while (!queue.isEmpty()) {
    List<Integer> parents = data.get(queue.poll());
    if (null == parents) {
      continue;
    }
    for (int parent : parents) {
      if (!ancestry.contains(parent)) {
        ancestry.add(parent);
        queue.add(parent);
      }
    }
  }
}
```

If the intersection of these sets is non-empty, then we are assured that the individuals are related. Putting this all together, the solution to the problem is given below.

Listing 8.6: Decide if Two People are Related

```
boolean related(Map<Integer, List<Integer>> data,
                int id1,
                int id2) {
  Set<Integer> ancestry1 = new HashSet<Integer>();
  find_ancestry(data, id1, ancestry1);
  Set<Integer> ancestry2 = new HashSet<Integer>();
  find_ancestry(data, id2, ancestry2);
  ancestry1.retainAll(ancestry2);
  return !ancestry1.isEmpty();
}
```

The listing above is not efficient, but it does solve the problem. Speaking to efficiency, it requires a full *bfs* traversal of the ancestry of one individual before beginning the second. Since the number of parents grows exponentially in a full family tree, the set of ancestors has the possibility of being extremely large. There are many ways to overcome this problem, such as a level traversal of the ancestry graph.

8.3 Depth first search

Depth first search is a graph traversal algorithm characterized by its use of a stack to maintain the frontier of traversal. We often abbreviate it as *dfs*. There are many important differences with *bfs*. Depth first search attempts to discover the next longest path, while breadth first search iterates through a frontier of equidistant nodes. Further, for each vertex visited in depth first search the stack maintains a path from that node to the root of the search. In *dfs*, the order of traversal history is lost when the next node is visited.

As with *bfs*, an implementation of *dfs* requires maintaining a list of vertices that have been visited. There are implicitly two such lists. The nodes on the stack will have their children visited, and the nodes already visited will never again be elements of the stack.

Listing 8.7: Depth First Search

```
void dfs(Node origin, Visitor visit) {
  Set<Node> queued = new HashSet<Node>();
  Stack<Node> stack = new Stack<Node>();
  stack.push(origin);
  queued.add(origin);
  while (!stack.isEmpty()) {
    Node current = stack.pop();
    for (Node neighbor : current.neighbors) {
      if (!queued.contains(neighbor)) {
        queued.add(neighbor);
        stack.push(neighbor);
      }
    }
    visit.visit(current);
  }
}
```

The listing could be simplified with recursion. Instead of maintaining the iterators in the stack, we could call *dfs* with the current `Node` as the origin. However we provide an iterative stack implementation to show the similarity with *bfs*. Notice that aside from using a stack instead of queue the code is similar. However, surprisingly different behavior results from such a small change from *bfs*.

8.3.1 Determine execution order of a task

Given a graphical representation of sub-processes of a large task, where each node in the graph represents a sub-process. The children of a node depend on the completion of their parent. The problem is to determine an execution order for all the processes in which no process is started before its parents have completed. For this problem the directed graph is special in that it has no cycles, and is called a directed acyclic graph. If it had cycles, then no sequential execution order would exist.

This problem of determining sequential execution order can be solved by *dfs*. Suppose the origin is a node that has no incoming edges. If we begin *dfs* from this node, because there are no cycles we will eventually reach a node that has no children. This node represents a process that is dependent upon the entire contents of the stack during *dfs*. We save this to the back of a list holding the reverse of execution order.

We continue in this fashion until every node is visited and added to the list. If the graph has not been fully traversed but *dfs* has an empty stack, we choose the next node from the graph with no incoming edges and iterate.

When this process completes, the list contains the reverse of the execution order. Reversing the list, we then have execution order.

The following listing implements the determination of execution order of the graph starting with `origin`. In this listing we assume there is exactly one node with no incoming edges, and that node is provided as the parameter. Since our implementation of *dfs* takes a `Visitor` parameter, the code is simplified by using an implementation of `Visitor`.

Listing 8.8: Dependency graph

```
class TopologicalSortVisitor implements Visitor {
  private List<Node> list;

  TopologicalSortVisitor(List<Node> list) {
    this.list = list;
  }

  public void visit(Node node) {
    list.add(node);
  }
}

void topological_sort(Node origin,
                      List<Node> list) {
  Visitor visit = new TopologicalSortVisitor(list);
  dfs(origin, visit);
  Collections.reverse(list);
}
```

It is worth noting that this problem is a specialization of the general problem of topologically sorting nodes in a directed graph, and has many other applications such as classifying nodes in connected components.

8.3.2 Find cycles in a graph

Suppose we are given a graph of nodes represented as an adjacency list, the question is to determine if there exist any cycles in the graph. Depth first search visits nodes by following edges. An edge that is traversed is called a tree edge. When *dfs* attempts to visit an element that is already on the stack, that edge is called a back-edge. Such an edge provides positive identification of a cycle, as it loops back to a path already traversed. So the problem of determining if a graph contains a cycle is as simple as finding a single back-edge in a *dfs*.

Finding a cycle is simplified if `Visitor` is provided the stack when called. However, this is not necessary. Consider the first node provided to `Visitor`. If this node has any children, then a cycle exists, else that child would have been added to the stack and visited first. Likewise, if any node is visited in which some child has not been previously visited then a cycle exists. With this intuition, we can quickly develop a solution.

Listing 8.9: Detect Cycles

```
class DetectCycleVisitor implements Visitor {
  boolean cycleDetected;
  private Set<Node> visited;

  DetectCycleVisitor(Boolean cycle_detected,
                     Set<Node> visited) {
    this.cycleDetected = cycle_detected;
    this.visited = visited;
  }

  public void visit(Node node) {
    visited.add(node);
    for (Node neighbor : node.neighbors) {
      if (visited.contains(neighbor)) {
        cycleDetected = true;
      }
    }
  }
}

boolean detect_cycle(Node origin) {
  Set<Node> visited = new HashSet<Node>();
  Visitor visit = new DetectCycleVisitor(
    false,
    visited);
  dfs(origin, visit);
  return ((DetectCycleVisitor)visit).cycleDetected;
}
```

When a cycle is detected by the presence of a back-edge, memoizing the tree edges and reconstructing the cycle from the paths from the origin to the first node in which a cycle was found could determine the nodes of the cycle.

Reconstructing a cycle is not much more involved. When the first cycle is detected, the `Visitor` would begin looking for tree edges that connect to either the head or tail of a partially constructed cycle. When an edge matches the head, it should be pushed to the front. When an edge originates at the tail, it is pushed back. When the head and tail are equal, a cycle has been found.

8.3.3 Find all the words in a boggle game

Let's consider a boggle board, defined as a two dimensional array of characters.

Listing 8.10: Definition of a Boggle Board

```
class GameBoard {
  char[][] board;

  GameBoard(char[][] board) {
    this.board = board;
  }

  int getNumRows() {
    return board.length;
  }

  int getNumCols() {
    return board[0].length;
  }
}
```

Each position is defined by a set of coordinates on the board. In the following list for `Position`, we also override the `hashCode` and `equals` methods so that we can compare `Position` objects by their coordinates later on.

Listing 8.11: Definition of a Position on the Board

```
class Position {
  int x;
  int y;

  Position(int x, int y) {
    this.x = x;
    this.y = y;
  }

  public int hashCode() {
    return x + y;
  }

  public boolean equals(Object obj) {
    if (!(obj instanceof Position)) {
      return false;
    }
    if (obj == this) {
      return true;
    }
    Position other = (Position)obj;
    return x == other.x && y == other.y;
  }
}
```

The $n \times n$ game board contains a single letter in each square. The question is to find all words that are simple paths in the graph represented by the matrix. In this graph, elements of the matrix are neighbors if they are above, below, left, right or diagonal. The problem is complicated by the fact that words can start from any node in the graph and that all paths need to be checked.

To solve this problem, we require an `is_word` function that returns true if a word has been found. We output each word found during the traversal that satisfies this function.

With this method available, let's begin by translating a matrix M given as a two dimensional array of characters into a directed graph. We begin by modifying `dfs` to the matrix to look for all neighbors. Neighbors are in any adjacent entry. Since we want all paths, we do not use the `queued` variable. But we do not want to backtrack on the stack, so instead of verifying that we have pushed a `Node` onto the stack, we only verify that the `Node` is not currently on the stack.

The following listing enumerates all words that can begin at a node in the graph.

Listing 8.12: Word Search in a Matrix from a Single Point

```
void boggle_dfs(GameBoard board,
                Set<String> words,
                Set<Position> visited,
                Position pos,
                StringBuilder word) {
  for (int row_offset = -1;
       row_offset <= 1;
       row_offset++) {
    for (int col_offset = -1;
         col_offset <= 1;
         col_offset++) {
      Position next_pos = new Position(
        pos.x + row_offset,
        pos.y + col_offset);
      if (next_pos.x < board.getNumRows()
          && next_pos.x >= 0
          && next_pos.y < board.getNumCols()
          && next_pos.y >= 0
          && !visited.contains(next_pos)) {
        visited.add(next_pos);
        word.append(
          board.board[next_pos.x][next_pos.y]);
        if (is_word(word.toString())) {
          words.add(word.toString());
        }
        boggle_dfs(board,
                   words,
                   visited,
                   next_pos,
                   word);
        visited.remove(next_pos);
        word.setLength(word.length() - 1);
      }
    }
  }
}

void boggle(GameBoard board,
            Position pos,
            Set<String> words) {
  Set<Position> visited = new HashSet<Position>();
  StringBuilder word = new StringBuilder();
  boggle_dfs(board, words, visited, pos, word);
}
```

This problem is unlike our previous examples where we traversed from a single starting point. To this end we must attempt multiple traversals, one for each node in the graph. So using the previous listing, the following function provides a complete solution to the problem.

Listing 8.13: Word Search in a Matrix

```
void boggle(GameBoard board, Set<String> words) {
  for (int row = 0;
       row < board.getNumRows();
       row++) {
    for (int col = 0;
         col < board.getNumCols();
         col++) {
      boggle(board,
             new Position(row, col),
             words);
    }
  }
}
```

8.4 $A^\star$ Search

We conclude graphical search with a brief example of $A^\star$ search. $A^\star$ search is a graphical search which uses a priority queue to order the frontier of exploration. The value of a node in the priority queue can be given by a heuristic measurement of the distance to a goal. In this way it differs from both *bfs* and *dfs* in that the order in which the nodes are to be visited are not fixed by the order in which they are discovered.

Suppose we are given maze represented by a square $n \times n$ matrix defined as a `GameBoard`. We are given a start position and an end position. The question is to write a function that produces a path through the maze.

To begin we refer to each position in the maze as coordinates, and a `passable` function determines whether or not a given node is passable. Only positions above, below, left, and right are neighbors. Neighbors that are passable are adjacent to a position in the board.

Now to solve the problem efficiently with $A^\star$ search, we would like to visit each node in order of its distance from the exit of the maze. The hope is that positions closer to the exit will have shorter paths to the exit.

However, if we knew the actual distance we could solve the problem by traversing from the exit to the start. Instead we use the heuristic that we want to visit the next node that is closest to the exit of the maze where distance is measured as if there is always a path directly from the node to the exit. So to apply $A^\star$ search, we will define a function which calculates the shortest possible distance between a position in the maze and the exit. While many metrics are available, we use Manhattan distance as our maze distance.

Listing 8.14: Admissible Maze Distance Heuristic

```
int distance(Position begin, Position end) {
  return Math.abs(begin.x - end.x)
         + Math.abs(begin.y - end.y);
}
```

Let us also define the following object to represent a position in the maze and the distance between it and the exit.

Listing 8.15: Definition of `DistancePosition`

```
class DistancePosition {
  int distance;
  Position position;

  DistancePosition(int distance,
                   Position position) {
    this.distance = distance;
    this.position = position;
  }
}
```

In solving the maze, we being at the start and continue as with `dfs` by iteratively constructing a path. However we use a priority queue instead of stack, where the distance heuristic gives the priority of a node. Nodes are considered in lowest priority value first. When the path reaches the exit, the path through the maze is reconstructed and the function terminates. If no solution exists, we return an empty path.

Listing 8.16: Search Through a Maze

```
void maze(GameBoard maze,
          Position start,
          Position exit,
          List<Position> route) {
  List<Position> offsets = Arrays.asList(
    new Position(-1, 0), new Position(1, 0),
    new Position(0, -1), new Position(0, 1));
  Map<Position, Position> parent =
    new HashMap<Position, Position>();
  PriorityQueue<DistancePosition> priority_queue =
    new PriorityQueue<DistancePosition>(
      maze.getNumRows() * maze.getNumCols(),
      new Comparator<DistancePosition>() {
        public int compare(DistancePosition a,
                           DistancePosition b) {
          return a.distance - b.distance;
        }
      });
  priority_queue.add(new DistancePosition(
    distance(start, exit), start));
  parent.put(start, start);
  while (!priority_queue.isEmpty()) {
    Position current =
      priority_queue.peek().position;
    if (exit.equals(current)) {
      do {
        route.add(0, current);
        current = parent.get(current);
      } while (current != start);
      route.add(0, start);
      return;
    }
    priority_queue.poll();
    for (Position offset : offsets) {
      Position neighbor = new Position(
        current.x + offset.x,
        current.y + offset.y);
      if (neighbor.x < maze.getNumRows()
          && neighbor.x >= 0
          && neighbor.y < maze.getNumCols()
          && neighbor.y >= 0
          && !parent.containsKey(neighbor)
          && passable(maze, neighbor)) {
        parent.put(neighbor, current);
        priority_queue.add(new DistancePosition(
          distance(neighbor, exit), neighbor));
      }
    }
  }
}
```

Notice that as with the boggle question, we use a static set of offsets to choose the next position in the maze. However since diagonal positions are not adjacent we have a restricted set of offsets. The `parent` variable serves two purposes; it is used to determine if a position has already been queued and it is used in reconstruction of the path. Finally, notice the usage of the `PriorityQueue` class where we pass to the constructor a custom `Comparator` that orders the elements by distance. While this question had a longer solution than most, the basic framework is similar to that of *bfs* and *dfs*.

Chapter 9

Selection

Selection is the last type of search we investigate.

In programming, we define the median of an array in terms of the sorted order of the array. The median of an array of n values is the value of the element at index $n/2$ in sorted order. That is if an array of values is ordered, the median is the value of the middle element. Although this definition is not the same as the statistical median, it is commonly useful in programming.

Selection is a generalization of the problem of finding the median. Concretely, selection is the problem of finding the kth median of an array A of n elements. That is the element x such that there are at least $k-1$ elements in A which are less than or equal to x, and $n-k$ elements of A greater than or equal to x

As is often the case with algorithms, it is just as easy to handle the general case of selection as it is to handle the specific case of finding the median. In the following we will see that doing so does not harm run time efficiency. It is just as efficient to find the element in the kth position of a sorted array as it is to find the median of an array when the values in the array can be unbounded.

In this section we will provide a progression of solutions for the problem of selection. We begin with selection through sorting, which is a simple but inefficient solution to the problem. We then look at a randomized selection algorithm, and improve it to deterministic bounds. We then conclude with a selection algorithm designed to operate over large data sets, a problem commonly asked at Google and Microsoft.

9.1 Selection through sort

The simplest approach to selection is to pre-sort the array, and return the element that resides in the kth position. Using the built-in `Arrays_sort` utility function, the method is simple to implement.

Listing 9.1: Selection by Sorting

```
int select(int[] array, int k) {
  Arrays.sort(array);
  return array[k];
}
```

An implementation of the median from this method is simple. Recall both that arrays are 0-indexed and, from our definition above, that we want the rightmost of two middle elements.

Listing 9.2: Median by Sorting

```
int median(int[] array) {
  return select(array, (array.length - 1) / 2);
}
```

This method always returns the correct answer, and it is hard to improve in terms of brevity. However it requires a full sort of the data. This turns out to be inefficient, as selection doesn't require the full sort order. Instead we only need to know whether or not there are k smaller elements in the array. In order to improve the run time, we first look at the problem of finding a proper pivot for which to partition instead of pre-sorting.

9.2 The pivot and partition operation

In binary search, we were able to cut the search space in half by knowing that every element with an index lower than the probe's was smaller than the probe, and every element with an index higher than the probe's was larger than the probe. Finding a good pivot element will allow similar narrowing of the search space in selection.

This is achieved by pivoting an array on an element that is close to the median. Given a value and an array, the pivot operation leaves the array in a state where every element of the array smaller than the pivot precedes it, and every element in the array larger than the pivot succeeds it.

There are many methods of implementing a partition on an array. One could use a list and push back larger values and push front smaller values.

The following listing partitions the sub-array defined by the offset and length on the value provided. The algorithm used initializes the array with the pivot element in the first position. It then enumerates the array from right to left. When an entry with value less than the pivot is detected, the tail of the array is shifted to the right of the pivot. That smaller value is then stored in the empty location created by the shift.

The return value is an index into the array. Every element of the array which is less than or equal to the pivot has a lower index than the return value. Every element that is greater than the pivot value has an index no less than the return value.

Listing 9.3: Partition on an Element

```
int partition(int[] array,
              int pos,
              int offset,
              int length) {
  if (length <= 1) {
    return offset;
  }
  int val = array[pos];
  array[pos] = array[offset];
  array[offset] = val;

  int left = offset;
  int right = offset + length - 1;
  while (left < right) {
    if (val < array[right]) {
      right--;
    } else {
      int tmp = array[left + 1];
      array[left + 1] = array[left];
      array[left] = tmp;
      if (right != (left + 1)) {
        array[left] = array[right];
        array[right] = tmp;
      }
      left++;
    }
  }
  return left;
}
```

The use of the left starting position and the size on which to pivot will be helpful in the sequel. We can now implement and analyze selection by choosing an arbitrary pivot.

9.3 Selection with a pivot

We begin with a rule to choose a pivot. We suppose a rule is declared as below. The parameters define the sub-array from which to choose a pivot.

Listing 9.4: Definition of Find Pivot Index

```
abstract int pivot_index(int[] array,
                         int offset,
                         int size);
```

Given a rule to choose a pivot, implementing selection can be done recursively. A partition operation first provides the sort location of the pivot element. If the desired location k is lower than the location of the pivot, we exclude all elements of the array from the pivot to the end. If the desired location is higher than the location of the pivot, we exclude all elements with indices smaller than the pivot and update k. We finally recursively apply selection to the range of the array not excluded.

Listing 9.5: Selection with Pivot

```
int select_with_pivot(int[] array,
                      int offset,
                      int length,
                      int k) {
  int index = pivot_index(array, offset, length);
  int pos = partition(array,
                      index,
                      offset,
                      length);
  if (pos == k) {
    return array[k];
  }
  if (pos > k) {
    return select_with_pivot(array,
                             offset,
                             pos - offset,
                             k);
  }
  return select_with_pivot(array,
                           pos + 1,
                           length
                             - (pos + 1 - offset),
                           k);
}

int select_with_pivot(int[] array, int k) {
  return select_with_pivot(array, 0,
                           array.length,
                           k);
}
```

This implementation would have expected linear running time over input provided uniformly at random. The reason is that we can expect to exclude half the size of the list with every pivot. However the run time is not guaranteed because the pivot may not provide a strong separation of the search space. In the worst case, where the array is sorted this implementation runs in quadratic time. The problem is the choice of element on which to pivot.

To provide a linear running time selection algorithm, we chose as a pivot the *median of the medians.*

9.4 Median of medians

The problem at hand is to guarantee that the choice of the pivot element separates the array into two pieces each with length at least some constant fraction of the original array. This could be done if we could always choose the median. But that is our goal, and we do not have that tool available. None-the-less, it is possible to choose an approximation of the median by reducing this original problem to a smaller problem. The following solution is called the median-of-medians or median-of-three .

The reduction works by first bucketing the array into sub-arrays of constant length. From each sub-array we can find a median value, which is simple if each bucket is of a constant length. A short listing for length of three makes this clear.

Listing 9.6: Median of 3

```
int median_of_3(int[] array,
                int offset,
                int length) {
  int[] sub = Arrays.copyOfRange(array,
                                 offset,
                                 offset + length);
  Arrays.sort(sub);
  return sub[(length - 1) / 2];
}
```

Choosing the median value of these medians will give us a value that is guaranteed to not be too far from the original actual median of the array. Analysis shows that the pivot chosen is approximately the median. Hence the running time of this process is linear to the length of the original arrays.

Implementing this algorithm is an exercise in recursion. We first bucket the array into sub-arrays of length 3, calculate the median of these three elements, and generate a new array consisting of these medians. Afterward we recursively find the median of the new array until it is small enough to decide in constant time.

Note the implementation operates on values, and then afterward find the index of the discovered value. The code can be changed to operate on indices, but doing so comes at the loss of some readability.

Listing 9.7: Median of Medians

```
int find_index(int[] array, int offset, int val) {
  int index = offset;
  while (val != array[index]) {
    index++;
  }
  return index;
}

int median_of_medians(int[] array,
                      int offset,
                      int length) {
  if (length <= 3) {
    return find_index(array,
                      offset,
                      median_of_3(array,
                                  offset,
                                  length));
  }
  int num = (length / 3)
          + ((length % 3) > 0 ? 1 : 0);
  int[] medians = new int[num];
  for (int step = 0; step < num; step++) {
    int index = step * 3;
    medians[step] =
      median_of_3(array,
                  offset + index,
                  Math.min(3, length - index));
  }
  return find_index(array,
                    offset,
                    median(medians));
}
```

With this we have an optimally efficient implementation of the selection algorithm. Interviewers often ask for pieces of the above and allow the candidate to continue through the problem as time permits.

A common generalization asks for an implementation of selection over a large data set.

9.5 Selection on large data

A difficult interview question, and usually a follow-up to a discussion of the selection problem, is to find the median on a large amount of data. The problem is stated that the data is too large to fit in memory and that it is desirable to avoid iterating through all the data in sequence.

To overcome the memory limitation problem we break the data up into separate arrays, requiring the candidate to operate over many small lists. The problem then reduces to finding a candidate median in a sub-array and determining that element's position in the overall data. If the median is not an element of one list, search must continue on the next array. As we can see, this question has become both a selection problem and a binary search problem.

In the listings in this section we provide a solution for finding the median of an arbitrary number of arrays. We first search the first array, and failing to find the median value the next is searched.

For clarity we separate out a number of initialization and ancillary functions.

As with binary search over multiple lists, a set of bounds for search must be associated with each list. To accomplish this, we define a class that holds a reference to a list, an offset associated with that list, and the length of each array to search. Together, the offset and length determine the lower and upper bounds for binary search. These items are called `ArrayBounds`.

Listing 9.8: Definition of **ArrayBounds** in Selection on Large Data

```
class ArrayBounds {
  int[] array;
  int offset;
  int length;

  ArrayBounds(int[] array,
              int offset,
              int length) {
    this.array = Arrays.copyOf(array,
                               array.length);
    this.offset = offset;
    this.length = length;
  }
}
```

We initialize the list of ArrayBounds objects using the following method.

Listing 9.9: Initialization for Selection on Large Data

```
int initialize_data(int[][] arrays,
                    List<ArrayBounds> data) {
  int total_size = 0;
  for (int[] array : arrays) {
    data.add(new ArrayBounds(array,
                             0,
                             array.length));
    total_size += array.length;
  }
  return total_size;
}
```

In our solution we must distinguish between the position of an element in an array and its index. The reason for this is that if we find that a value is in the first position of n lists, it is also in the nth overall position. However the sum of the indices is 0. We distinguish between 0-based indices and 1-based position counters by variable name.

We shall also see that we must pivot over a value that may not be in the array. In order to properly update the search bounds, we must be able to know whether or not the pivot operation encountered the pivot value. Pivot information is stored in the following data type. The `position` entry is the position of the pivot and `found` is whether or not the pivot value was encountered in partitioning.

Listing 9.10: Definition of `Pivot` in Selection on Large Data

```
class Pivot {
  int position;
  boolean found;

  Pivot(int position, boolean found) {
    this.position = position;
    this.found = found;
  }
}
```

`nth_element` finds the nth element in the array and rearranges the elements within the range in such a way that elements to the left of n are lesser and elements to the right of n are greater than n.

Listing 9.11: Find the nth Element in an Array

```
void nth_element(int[] data,
                 int begin,
                 int end,
                 int k) {
  int endIndex = end - 1;
  while (begin < endIndex) {
    int i = begin;
    int j = endIndex;
    int mid = data[(i + j) / 2];
    while (i < j) {
      if (data[i] >= mid) {
        int temp = data[j];
        data[j] = data[i];
        data[i] = temp;
        j--;
      } else {
        i++;
      }
    }

    if (data[i] > mid) {
      i--;
    }
    if (k <= i) {
      endIndex = i;
    } else {
      begin = i + 1;
    }
  }
}
```

With the pre-amble concluded, the following listing is the main loop of a solution for the median of large data. It takes each array in turn and determines if the median is a member of that list. This is accomplished by doing a binary search over the bounds of each list and finding the location of that element's value within the remaining lists.

Listing 9.12: Median of Large Data

```
int median(int[][] arrays) {
  List<ArrayBounds> data =
    new ArrayList<ArrayBounds>();
  int total_size = initialize_data(arrays, data);
  int median_pos = (total_size - 1) / 2 + 1;
  int pos_offset = 0;
  for (int data_index = 0;
       data_index < data.size();
       data_index++) {
    ArrayBounds tuple = data.get(data_index);
    while (0 != tuple.length) {
      int mid_index = tuple.offset
                      + tuple.length / 2;
      nth_element(tuple.array,
                  tuple.offset,
                  tuple.offset + tuple.length,
                  mid_index);
      int value = tuple.array[mid_index];
      int mid_pos = pos_offset + mid_index + 1;
      List<Pivot> pivots = new ArrayList<Pivot>();
      pivots.add(new Pivot(mid_index, true));
      partition_array_on_pivot(data_index,
                               value,
                               data,
                               pivots,
                               mid_pos);
      if (mid_pos == median_pos) {
        return value;
      }
      update_search_bounds(median_pos,
                           mid_pos,
                           data_index,
                           data,
                           pivots);
    }
    pos_offset += tuple.offset;
  }
  ArrayBounds tuple = data.get(data.size() - 1);
  return tuple.array[tuple.offset];
}
```

Two methods used in the solution have not yet been introduced: `partition_array_on_pivot` and `update_search_bounds`. The `partition_array_on_pivot` method pivots all other lists on the value being considered for the median in the current list. It uses the following `partition_around_value` method to partition an array around a given element.

Listing 9.13: Partition an Array Around a Given Value

```
int partition_around_value(int[] array,
                           int begin,
                           int end,
                           int value) {
  while (begin != end) {
    while (value > array[begin]) {
      begin++;
      if (begin == end) {
        return begin;
      }
    }
    do {
      end--;
      if (begin == end) {
        return begin;
      }
    } while (value <= array[end]);
    int temp = array[begin];
    array[begin] = array[end];
    array[end] = temp;
  }
  return begin;
}
```

`partition_array_on_pivot` first separates values above and below the pivot value. It then checks the minimum value of that partition to see if the pivot is a member of the upper partition.

Listing 9.14: Partition Array on Pivot

```
void partition_array_on_pivot(
    int index,
    int value,
    List<ArrayBounds> data,
    List<Pivot> pivots,
    Integer next_pos) {
  for (int offset = 1;
       (offset + index) < data.size();
       offset++) {
    int data_index = index + offset;
    ArrayBounds tuple = data.get(data_index);
    int begin = tuple.offset;
    int end = begin + tuple.length;
    int pos = partition_around_value(
      tuple.array,
      begin,
      end,
      value);
    boolean found_value = false;
    if (end != pos) {
      nth_element(tuple.array, pos, end, pos);
      if (value == tuple.array[pos]) {
        found_value = true;
      }
    }
    pivots.add(new Pivot(pos, found_value));
    Pivot last = pivots.get(pivots.size() - 1);
    next_pos += (tuple.offset
      + last.position
      + (last.found ? 1 : 0));
  }
}
```

The second method is `update_search_bounds` which updates the search bounds for every list. The update is based on whether the over-all median is less than or greater than the considered value. It is during this update that the binary search is affected on the current list.

Listing 9.15: Update Search Bounds After Partition

```
void update_search_bounds(int target_pos,
                          int current_pos,
                          int data_index,
                          List<ArrayBounds> data,
                          List<Pivot> pivots) {
  for (int offset = 0;
       (offset + data_index) < data.size();
       offset++) {
    ArrayBounds tuple = data.get(
      data_index + offset);
    if (current_pos <= target_pos) {
      tuple.length -= (pivots.get(offset).position
                       - tuple.offset);
      tuple.offset = pivots.get(offset).position;
      if (0 == offset) {
        tuple.offset++;
        tuple.length--;
      }
    } else {
      tuple.length = (pivots.get(offset).position
                      - tuple.offset);
    }
  }
}
```

All together, these methods provide a complete solution. The main idea of combining selection and binary search is presented in the main loop. And it is that which is often the insight required for solving this problem.

Chapter 10

Sorting

Sorting is a fundamental task in programming, and no one should be taken off guard when asked to sort a collection of integers or strings. One should be able to produce a number of optimal sorts from memory. This means not only avoiding quadratic sorts, but also choosing appropriately between quick sort, merge sort, radix sort, and others depending on the problem constraints.

All optimal sorts have worst case run times of order $n \log n$ over unbounded data. Insertion sort is often used for small data sets, but it has quadratic worst case running time. It should be avoided unless the problem is explicitly constrained so that it is efficient. Otherwise the only quadratic sorting algorithm you should ever give in an interview is quick sort. And even with a naive quick sort implementation, you should be able to explain that in its basic implementation it has order $n \log(n)$ running time in expectation, but can be made to have deterministic order $n \log(n)$ running time with a clever choice of pivots.

In this chapter we will implement five sorting algorithms and discuss their comparative merits. These algorithms are insertion sort, heap sort, quick sort, radix sort, and merge sort.

10.1 Insertion sort

Insertion sort is an inefficient sort that is practical for small data sets or data sets with only a small perturbation from sorted order.

Insertion sort works by iteratively inserting each element of an array into its proper position in a sorted sub-array. A standard implementation has an outer loop and an inner loop. The outer loop visits each value of an array from front to back, leaving behind a sorted sub-array. The inner loop searches for the position of the outer loop value in the sorted sub-array by scanning from back to front. During this search a portion of the sorted sub-array is shifted right one position, and the value is inserted into the vacated position.

Listing 10.1: Insertion Sort

```
void insertion_sort(int[] array) {
  for (int i = 1; i < array.length; i++) {
    int val = array[i];
    for (int j = i - 1;
         j >= 0 && array[j] > val;
         j--) {
      int tmp = array[j];
      array[j] = array[j + 1];
      array[j + 1] = tmp;
    }
  }
}
```

As can be seen, insertion sort is an in-place algorithm as it does not require allocation of memory from the heap. Insertion sort is also a stable sort, as the algorithm maintains the relative order of elements. Lastly, as only the indices and a temporary value are required insertion sort requires constant extra space.

The main drawback is that insertion sort has quadratic worst case behavior. Our next algorithm overcomes this drawback.

10.2 Heap sort

Heap sort uses a priority queue to achieve optimal worst case running time for a sort.

Heap-sort operates as follows. We create a max heap using the a `PriorityQueue`. Afterward, max values are iteratively removed and stored in their proper location in a partially sorted sub-array at the tail end of the array. Recalling that creating a heap is an order $n \log n$ operation and removing the first element in a heap is a logarithmic time operation called once for each element in the array, we can see that heap sort is an optimal sort.

Listing 10.2: Heap Sort

```
void heap_sort(int[] array) {
  PriorityQueue<Integer> heap =
    new PriorityQueue<Integer>(array.length);
  for (int value : array) {
    heap.add(value);
  }
  for (int i = 0; i < array.length; i++) {
    array[i] = heap.poll();
  }
}
```

Since building the heap and removing the max require no external memory, heap sort is an in-place algorithm. Since the heap creation may shuffle the relative locations of elements, heap-sort is not a stable sort. And lastly, from our implementation of the in-place heapify method we can see that heap sort uses constant space.

10.3 Quick sort

Quick sort is a divide and conquer algorithm that, like selection, partitions the data on a properly chosen pivot and recursively operates on the sub-arrays produced.

With a random pivot selection, quick sort provides expected optimal run time. However the worst case run time is quadratic. This is overcome by choosing a pivot element that is near the median of the array. The implementation of median-of-3 provided in the section on selection would suffice to guarantee optimal worst case behavior. Instead, we use the linear time `nth_element` pivot selection method presented earlier which is modified and reimplemented here for convenience. Using `nth_element` will increase effective run time, but the worst case asymptotic bound in unaffected.

Listing 10.3: Quick Sort

```
void quick_sort(int[] array) {
  quick_sort(array, 0, array.length - 1);
}

void quick_sort(int[] array, int low, int high) {
  if ((high - low) < 1) {
    return;
  }
  int mid = (low + high) / 2;
  int i = low;
  int j = high;
  while (i <= j) {
    while (array[i] <= array[mid] && i < mid) {
      i++;
    }
    while (array[j] > array[mid]) {
      j--;
    }
    if (i <= j) {
      int temp = array[i];
      array[i] = array[j];
      array[j] = temp;
      i++;
      j--;
    }
  }
  if (j > low) {
    quick_sort(array, low, j);
  }
  if (i < high) {
    quick_sort(array, i, high);
  }
}
```

As seen in our study of selection, finding the median element is an in-place operation. Partitioning and sub-array recursing are also in-place, and hence quick sort is an in-place sort. Further, if `nth_element` is stable, then so is quick sort. Lastly, note that quick sort uses only a constant amount of extra space.

For these reasons quick sort is often the best generic sorting algorithm to use in applications.

10.4 Radix sort

In radix sort, values are first bucketed by the value of some digit prior to merging. By bucketing over more than two sets, radix sort is a generalization of quick sort. For input from a bounded set, radix sort achieves linear time worst case behavior. However this run time falls back to quadratic when the input is from an unbounded domain.

Radix sort can be implemented on any radix; for instance binary digits or decimal digits. Below we implement radix sort on hexadecimal digit representations of integers.

Listing 10.4: Radix Sort

```
void radix_sort(int[] array) {
  List<List<Integer>> buckets =
    new ArrayList<List<Integer>>(0xf + 1);
  for (int i = 0; i < (0xf + 1); i++) {
    buckets.add(new ArrayList<Integer>());
  }
  for (int i = 0; i < 4; i++) {
    long offset = i * 4;
    long mask = 0xf << offset;
    for (int val : array) {
      int bucket = (int) ((mask & val) >> offset);
      buckets.get(bucket).add(val);
    }
    int index = 0;
    for (List<Integer> bucket : buckets) {
      for (Integer val : bucket) {
        array[index++] = val;
      }
      bucket.clear();
    }
  }
}
```

Radix sort is only optimal for fixed length data, such as integers bounded by some maximum. In order to bucket the input, radix sort requires external memory and is not in-place. Radix sort is a stable sort, as the relative order of values is maintained through each iteration of the algorithm.

10.5 Merge sort

Merge sort is another divide-and-conquer algorithm for sorting. The idea springs from the observation that if one starts with two sorted sub-arrays, it is simple to combine them into a single sorted array. This can be done by first comparing the smallest elements of each array for the minimum. That element is removed from its current array and added to the result, and the process iterates. Since the original arrays are sorted, this involves only a linear scan. So all that is left is how to set up the smaller arrays. As with quick sort, we can always divide input into smaller halves until we are left with individual units. We can then combine these into sorted output.

Listing 10.5: Merge Sort

```
void merge_sort(int[] data) {
  if (data.length <= 1)
    return;
  int mid = data.length / 2;
  int[] left = Arrays.copyOfRange(data, 0, mid);
  merge_sort(left);
  int[] right = Arrays.copyOfRange(data,
                                  mid,
                                  data.length);
  merge_sort(right);
  int index = 0;
  int left_index = 0;
  int right_index = 0;
  while (index < data.length) {
    if (left_index == left.length) {
      data[index] = right[right_index];
      right_index++;
    } else if (right_index == right.length) {
      data[index] = left[left_index];
      left_index++;
    } else if (left[left_index]
               < right[right_index]) {
      data[index] = left[left_index];
      left_index++;
    } else {
      data[index] = right[right_index];
      right_index++;
    }
    index++;
  }
}
```

As the merge is in-place, this implementation requires only memory allocation on the stack. However the recursive calls may require up to logarithmic extra space. Merge sort can be implemented as a stable sort.

While worst case behavior is asymptotically equivalent to that of quick sort, it has been argued that in-place quick sort is faster in practice. There are many possible reasons for this, including optimization of the inner loop of quick sort and lower stack space requirements. However, merge sort is the obvious choice when sorting over large data.

10.6 Sorting over large data

A favorite interview question at Google asks to sort 4GB of data using only 100MB of memory. While the specific numerical limits may change, the key insight is to use merge sort to accomplish sorting over large data.

This is an exercise in partitioning and merging. First, each contiguous sub-array of the smaller bound of data should be sorted with quick sort. Doing so is fast, in place, and requires only a constant amount of extra memory. Afterward, each of these sub-arrays is merged as with merge sort. A sample implementation of the merge is provided below.

Listing 10.6: Sorting Large Data with Merge Sort

```
void merge_arrays(List<List<Integer>> in,
                  List<Integer> out) {
  PriorityQueue<List<Integer>> heap =
    new PriorityQueue<List<Integer>>(in.size(),
      new Comparator<List<Integer>>() {
        public int compare(List<Integer> a,
                           List<Integer> b) {
          return a.get(0) - b.get(0);
        }
      });
  for (List<Integer> list : in) {
    if (null != list && !list.isEmpty()) {
      heap.add(list);
    }
  }
  while (!heap.isEmpty()) {
    List<Integer> list = heap.poll();
    out.add(list.remove(0));
    if (!list.isEmpty()) {
      heap.add(list);
    }
  }
}
```

Afterward

And with that, we complete this step in our journey. I hope you've enjoyed this tour through elementary data structures and fundamental algorithms. We've covered a lot of material and solved some of the most difficult problems encountered in technical interviews. I enjoyed the process of writing this book, and sincerely hope you enjoyed reading it. If you're new to computer programming, I hope you enjoyed learning the tricks and techniques the selection of problems covered. If you're an experienced developer, I hope this volume reminded you of the joy of solving problems that keeps us in engineering. Thanks for coming along with me, and I look forward to seeing you again in volume two, *Advanced Algorithms in* `Java`.

Index

$A^\star$ search, 121

binary heap, 60
binary search, 91
binary search tree, 28
- ancestry, 39
- balanced, 37
- depth, 35
- find, 29
- find parent, 30
- find successor, 31
- in-order traversal, 44
- insert, 28
- lowest common ancestor, 40
- post-order traversal, 44
- pre-order traversal, 44
- remove, 30, 32
- successor, 31
- traversal, 43

binary tree, 27
- size, 34

breadth first search, 106
Brodal heap, 60

cache, 88
collision resolution, 79
cuckoo hashing, 83
cycle, 106

depth first search, 112
Dijkstra, 108

edge, 105

Fibonacci heap, 60
fixed-point, 97

graph, 105
- adjacency list, 105
- connected, 106
- directed, 105
- undirected, 105

hash function, 72
hash table, 74
- collision resolution, 79
- dynamic resizing, 78
- find, 77
- insert, 77

heap, 59
- find_max, 63
- heap property, 59
- increase key, 64
- insert, 62
- max heap, 59
- min heap, 59
- remove_max, 63

heap sort, 144
histogram, 55

in-place, 144
insertion sort, 143

level order traversal, 53
linked lists, 7
- k^{th} from the end, 18
- circular, 11

- comparison, 20
- doubly, 14
- find, 9
- insertion, 8
- loops, 24
- merging, 21
- midpoint, 17
- palindrome, 22
- remove, 10
- remove values, 19
- reverse, 19
- selection, 16

Manhattan distance, 122
median, *see* selection
median-of-medians, 133
median-of-three, 133
merge sort, 148
most recently used cache, 88

open addressing, 81

path, 106
- simple, 106

queue, 47
- dequeue, 47
- enqueue, 47

quick sort, 145

radix sort, 147

selection, 127
- median, 127

separate chaining, 79
sorting, 143
- heap sort, 144
- insertion sort, 143
- merge sort, 148
- quick sort, 145
- radix sort, 147

stack, 48
- pop, 48
- push, 48

uniform distribution, 72

vertex, 105
- adjacent, 105
- neighbor, 105

Young tableau, 99

www.ingramcontent.com/pod-product-compliance
Lightning Source LLC
Chambersburg PA
CBHW071158050326
40689CB00011B/2158